Effective

Psychology

for Managers

Effective

Psychology

for Managers

Mortimer R. Feinberg, Ph.D.

*Professor of Psychology, Baruch School,
City University of New York
President, BFS Psychological Consultants, Inc.
Principal lecturer, American Management Association*

Englewood Cliffs, N. J. PRENTICE-HALL, INC.

A dedication:

This book is gratefully dedicated to three people. Two of them are now gone, and I miss them every day of my life.

> *To my mother Frieda, who still sets high standards for both her sons. This book is just one of the achievements in which she shares.*

> *To my father Max, whose memory is a blessing, and whose love and compassion sustain me.*

> *To my intellectual father, Dr. Douglas H. Fryer — teacher and guide.*

To all of them, this book is a small repayment for all they have given me.

Preface

An interesting story of significance to business management is told in the eighteenth chapter of Exodus. Moses, leader of all the Hebrews, is leading his people "out of the land of Pharaoh" when he is visited by his father-in-law Jethro.

Jethro quickly observes that Moses is a lonely and heavily burdened leader of many thousands of followers. More important, he is appalled at Moses' failure to select men capable of assisting him in his task, and at Moses' failure to delegate any authority and responsibility so as to share the burden.

"Hearken now unto my voice,'" says Jethro. "I will give thee counsel. The thing that thou doest is not good. Thou wilt surely wear away, for thou art not able to perform (*thy burden*) alone."

Having thus informed his son-in-law that he has acquired the services of a management consultant, Jethro suggests that Moses select some capable assistants from among his flock: "Thou shalt provide out of all the people able men, such as fear God, men of truth, hating unjust gain. Place them to be rulers of thousands, rulers of hundreds, rulers of fifties and rulers of tens," says Jethro. "And it shall be, that every great matter they shall bring unto thee, but every small matter they shall judge themselves. So shall they make it easier for thee and bear thy burden with thee."

This Biblical tale is the first recorded instance of management

7

sychology. With unique management insight, Jethro advises Moses to learn which of his men are capable of leading many people and which are capable of leading only a few; he further advises Moses to assign the men to appropriate tasks with appropriate authority to solve minor problems themselves, reserving for Moses only major decisions on significant matters. All this would make Moses' job less difficult.

Thus, in the space of just a few verses, Jethro has imparted the fundamental wisdom and logic behind personnel recruitment and selection, job placement, assignment of responsibility, delegation of authority, and other vital concerns of personnel management.

That same logic is still applicable today. But today's typical corporate manager, whether he is a production supervisor, middle-manager, or top executive must know much more about developing leaders, motivating people, persuading and counseling them, than did Moses or Jethro. In fact, the manager of today needs to know a tremendous amount of information about *himself* if he is to set himself up as leader, counselor and coach of others.

It is to this purpose that this book was written. It draws on my experience as a practicing management consultant to suggest ways of improving your own management techniques. It will teach you how to better counsel and coach the people who work for you — your assistants, your staff, your employees. These are the people who form the foundation of your success. Without their help, *you* cannot succeed.

Much of the material in this book is quoted or adapted from articles and reports for management which I originally wrote for publication by the Research Institute of America. I was chief psychologist at the Research Institute for five years, and it was during that period that I learned how to translate psychological insights into practical management recommendations. To *all* at the Institute, a tremendous debt is owed.

In addition, some chapters of the book are actually expanded versions or adaptations of articles which first appeared in the following business magazines: *Business Management, Nation's Business, Supervisory Management,* and *Dun's Review and Modern Industry.* To the editors of those publications, my sincere thanks for their help.

I owe a debt of gratitude to the following professional colleagues: Dr. Milton Sapirstein, Head of Organizational Psychiatry, Mount Sinai Hospital, New York; Dr. Paul M. Steinberg, Dean of Hebrew Union College, New York; Prof. Edward W. Arluck and Prof. Sheldon S. Zalkind, of the Baruch School of Business, City University of New York; and Prof. J. E. Barmack, Chairman of the Psychology Department, City University of New York. I also wish to acknowledge the contribution of Dr. Valentine Appel, Vice-president, Benton & Bowles, Inc. I owe a special debt to Dean Emanuel Saxe of the Baruch School, whose career has been an inspiration and a guide.

I also offer thanks to my colleagues at BFS Psychological Associates, particularly Dr. Benjamin Balinsky, Myron Katz, Lloyd Thorner, Dr. Lawrence Zeitlin, Dr. Irving Weisman, and my secretary, Elsie Quinn. They have willingly shared their insights and have demonstrated much patience with me.

A special thanks to my sister-in-law Mary Ellen Feinberg, whose clerical assistance speeded the completion of the manuscript. Also to Dr. Harvey B. Feinberg of Mt. Sinai Hospital who has been in the Biblical sense "his brother's keeper."

I acknowledge my friend and professional associate, Bernard Weiss, who assisted immensely in the editorial guidance of the manuscript. I am certain he gained some comfort in its completion.

Finally, to my treasured family—Gloria, my wife, Stuart and E. Todd, my sons, who permitted me the time away from them to finish this labor of love.

M. R. Feinberg

Contents

1.

How to Handle
the Ten Tough Tasks
Of a Boss

Face the fact, pure and simple—you can't change people.

Try as you might, you will never change a man's personality to make him conform to your conception of what he should be.

There are only three ways to change a man's personality. There's religious conversion, there's psychoanalysis, and there's brain surgery. Since you are neither a minister, a psychotherapist, nor a brain surgeon, you might as well stop wasting your time.

You are a manager in a tough, competitive business. Therefore, instead of vainly trying to "build" a staff, make the best of what you've got. Try to develop the potential that exists on your present staff. It must be there, or you wouldn't have hired those people in the first place.

In my personal observations of top executives, both good and not-so-good, I find that the most successful men are those who realize a basic, fundamental proposition: that they must work almost entirely within the framework of other peoples' strengths and weaknesses, abilities and deficiencies. They make the best of what they've got; they know how to handle people on their staff who, in turn, must handle people themselves.

The most mature managers—those who are most respected by their subordinates—recognize the individual differences among employees. They know that some men are vain, some are "pushy," some are too ambitious, some are maddeningly creative; while others are mentally weak, lazy, immature, or incompetent. However, the successful manager never tries to change these differences. On the contrary, he tries only to capitalize on his knowledge of subordinates. He plays not the role of God, but the role of the counselor and coach. He brings out the best of what his people have to offer; when the need is apparent, he is cold and without conscience in dismissing the hopeless cases.

How does this philosophy apply in a typical business situation? After sitting in on one of my recent lectures to a group of high-salaried executives, the managing editor of a national business magazine challenged me to apply these principles to 10 very difficult "people problems." The editor, questioning me as a company president would, probed for the solutions to "his problems" in two long tape-recorded interviews.

His article was subsequently published in *Business Management* Magazine (where it became one of the best-read stories of the year) and later appeared in the business section of the Chicago *Daily News.* I think you will find it to be practical common-sense advice, not psychological mumbo-jumbo, that will have lasting value. Here's how I responded to the "company president's" problems:

#1. HOW, AND UNDER WHAT CIRCUMSTANCES, SHOULD I GET INVOLVED IN A SUBORDINATE'S PERSONAL AFFAIRS?

Rarely should you get involved at all—at least, not until the man's work is being affected by his alcoholism, his extra-marital sex, or whatever. The path to many an employee's downfall is paved by his boss' good intentions.

You, as manager, must play the role of the industrial referee, saying, "These are the rules of the game. Here's how you get to first base; here's how you get to second base, third, and home." Now, as long as the subordinate is playing according to the rules, the referee isn't supposed to blow the whistle. But if the rules are broken, then the referee may cautiously intervene. The criterion is clear-cut: If the problem is interfering with the man's work, you can involve yourself. Otherwise, you must leave him alone. It makes no difference whether he's an executive or a file clerk.

But I want to be preventive. I want to prevent any interference before it occurs. What can I do?

I believe in prophylactic measures, but they won't work in cases like these. When the employee's personal problem is not interfering with his work, he feels you are meddling; he thinks he's got that problem under control. What's more, he may *need* his drinking or his extra-marital sex in order to keep functioning. A neurosis is an adjustment—inadequate, perhaps—but it's his adjustment in order to keep himself from becoming more seriously ill. And you certainly won't help him by saying, "Look, you're sick." You'll destroy him.

Never approach him on the moral level. If you feel you *must* get through to him somehow, approach him on an objective level. Use an objective argument: He's way over budget, he comes to work late, or he's endangering an important account. Gingerly approach him on this basis and say, "Look, I'm not here to probe into your personal affairs. I am not here to evaluate your life, to judge you or make any moral lectures. That's somebody else's job, not mine. And I can't help you as much as I would like. All I can tell you is that your sales volume has started to deteriorate (or your production level is starting to drop, or your staff is unhappy). Compared with the man you were, you are no longer that man. I don't *know* if it's the women you're seeing. All I'm telling you is that you're not hitting that ball like you used to. If this continues, I can't keep you on this team. I don't care if you are up all night with a woman or reading the Bible, all I know is that your late hours are interfering with the job."

I know of no single case in industry where a man with a deep emotional problem was helped by having a long heart-to-heart talk with his boss. You are not qualified to advise another man on his pathology. You may tell him to cut out sex in the office. But he won't; he'll just cover up his traces a little better. I actually saw this happen. A neurosis will not yield to a verbal pep-talk. If it would, you wouldn't have any problems, because we all get these pep-talks in church, in the synagogue, at the PTA—and from company presidents.

One other caution: Never try to reach such a man through his wife. She may repeat all the negative comments you make, and this can destroy him. There's an old Jewish expression: "When two heads lie on the same pillow, nothing should come between." Don't talk to an employee's wife about his problems. Besides, she probably already knows of them anyway!

What about professional help?

Good. Let him go to a therapist, but you're going to have to be patient. I've seen companies wait three to six months for a man to return to normal during therapy. You'd wait for him if he had a broken leg, wouldn't you? Psychological problems are in the same category as broken legs and broken arms—with one reservation: We may not be certain of therapy. It doesn't always work.

#2. HOW DO I FIRE A LONG-TIME ASSOCIATE, A GOOD FRIEND? WHAT DO I TELL HIM, AND HOW DO I BREAK THE BAD NEWS?

It's an impossible situation, and I have never seen anyone handle it well. Most of the time the president avoids the issue and continues to hang on to his friend. The president rationalizes: "My old friend has 25 years in the company. How can I do this to him?"

A poor manager keeps the executive in his old job and lets him die there. A better manager transfers his old friend to a position of less responsibility, putting him out to pasture, and prays for a resignation. The smart manager does the deed and gets it out of the way so he can worry about more important matters.

Firing an old friend is a bloody mess. It will make you sick, and you won't sleep well for weeks. But this is your job. How does a general respond when he has to send out a platoon knowing it isn't coming back? The general has to take the hill at all costs. He sacrifices the platoon in order to win the battle.

Many men won't accept high management positions because they don't want responsibility like this. Remember: These are command decisions. The survival of your company is in your hands. You are entrusted with your area of management, which is more important than one man's future. Also, it is highly possible that your friend will be happier somewhere else. Your company is *not* his last salvation.

When you fire him, make it short, make it sweet (offer to help him find another job, if he's capable), and don't criticize anything about his character or professional competence that he can't improve anyway.

My brother is a physician. When I ask him how he chooses a surgeon, he says he selects a man who is so certain of his knife, who gets in so fast and so deep, and gets out so fast, that there's almost no blood. That's the way to be with your old friend. Don't prolong the agony.

#3. WHAT IS THE MOST EFFECTIVE WAY TO PRAISE SUBORDINATES?

Managers often have real trouble in this area. They set such high standards for themselves that it's hard for them to praise others. The typical manager either over-does it or never does it.

First, avoid praising every little thing the man accomplishes. Frequent praise will quickly lose its desired effect and may even demotivate him. Save your praise for a particularly difficult task handled well. The former president of a clothing company had such a reputation for over-praising that one of his staff men used to say, "My head hurts from so much patting."

Second, don't exaggerate. People resent it, and you lose their respect. Let me quote a translation from *Art of Success* by Gracian, a Spanish Jesuit philosopher: "Exaggeration is an excess which reflects both on one's knowledge and one's taste. . . . The prudent man goes more cautiously and . . . prefers to err on the short rather than the long side. True excellence is rare. Do not belittle it by exaggeration. Exaggeration is a form of lying, and one loses by it the credit for good taste, which is much, and the credit for judgment, which is more." President Johnson knows what harm can come of excessive praise. Once, long ago, he was introduced with a lot of flowery compliments and doubted that the audience would swallow them. He stood up to speak and said, "My father would appreciate all those fine compliments, but only my mother would believe them!" So, praise with prudence.

On the other hand, you don't want to under-praise either. Don't be like the man who was celebrating his 50th wedding anniversary and hadn't said "I love you" to his wife since the day they were married. When his wife complained, he replied, "Dear, I told you 50 years ago 'I love you' and you know I'm a man who never goes back on his word!" This approach doesn't work in industry.

Finally, praise a man in the area of his anxiety—where he is trying to do a good job and where you know he feels he ought to be making some progress. Arturo Toscanini says that the greatest compliment ever paid him came from Marian Anderson. "She didn't rush up to me after the concert and say, 'Arturo, you conducted well.' By the age of 70, I knew I was a great conductor. She grabbed me by the hand, gave it a little squeeze, and said, 'Arturo, you looked *handsome* up there tonight.'" At 70 years of age, a man's appearance may well be the area of his anxiety.

Should praise be rendered in public?

Praise in the presence of others only if it is important that others know you have a high opinion of this man. This might be embarrassing to him, but he would be even more embarrassed if you didn't praise him at all.

Praising in public is dangerous. The critical period is when you've just appointed a man to a new job and you praise him in front of the people who will work for him. If you over-praise by just a little, the employees say, "Boy, this guy has got to be great." Later, they're disappointed. Or they'll say, "Eh, we've heard it all before," and they won't believe it. If you *under-praise*, the reaction is, "Say, I wonder if this new guy is really capable? Does he know what we're doing here?" Strike a medium with your praise, make it brief, and be specific.

#4. HOW CAN I TELL IF AN EXECUTIVE HAS REAL POTENTIAL FOR TOP MANAGEMENT? WHAT ARE THE SIGNS OF SUCCESS?

Let's dismiss the business and professional qualifications. I'll talk about personal characteristics.

The best corporate officers, the men who are recognized as tops, are characterized as having high drive, high energy expenditure; they do many different things simultaneously—not all of them well, necessarily—but they are *driven* people. Napoleon could do seven things at once. Look for such traits in your subordinates.

I have never seen a top executive who was passive, contemplative, "sicklied over with the pale cast of thought." Hamlet would never become a good executive, in my view. There may be some Hamlets around, but they aren't holding the top jobs. When Fred Friendly was named president of CBS News, *Time* Magazine stated that he is known in the industry as "Frenzied Fred" because "he expects others to tackle every project with his own clock-defying zeal." Carl Sandburg describes Friendly as always looking "as if he just got off a foam-flecked horse."

There are some other, more subtle characteristics, that distinguish the potential presidents from the also-rans on the executive staff:

1. *Dedication.* Just plain, sheer devotion. You call in the guy and you say, "Listen, Jack, you've got to fly to Chicago and get that order. Get out there tonight." Occasionally, he may have a good excuse—his wife is sick, or his kid is in the hospital. But if he goes 99% of the time, he is committed to the game of making your company successful.

2. *Competitiveness.* Good executives can't stand to lose. They are interested only in winning. They are constantly evaluating themselves against the competition and striving to do better at each opportunity. They change their frames of reference. One executive, a self-made man, told me when he was on the way up: "Here I am, sitting at the feet of the elephants, and I'm just a mouse. They might kill me. Just by accident. Because I'm a mouse and they are elephants." I asked him, "What are you going to do?" He said, "I'm gonna become an elephant, too."

3. *Honesty.* How honest is he with himself? Does he wear $250 suits and dirty underwear? Is he aware of some of his own limitations? How honest is he with you? How consistently does he produce what he said he would produce? Is his level of aspiration out of contact with reality, or is it close to what he can actually achieve? If he says, "OK, I didn't do too well that time, but I learned a lesson and I'll do better next time around," then he's honest with himself.

4. *Realism.* He has his feet on the ground. He doesn't just dream about how great he's going to be someday. If he's always seeing the big picture and never the details, he's in trouble. The good executive is looking at how he's going to get where he wants to be. He is almost compulsive about the little things, the short steps, the pennies.

5. *Maturity.* He knows that his own future rests on what happens to other people. He can fire a man who does not contribute to the well-being of the organization. He respects differences of opinion. He doesn't meddle in office politics and he refuses to manipulate people. He is patient. He doesn't accept the first solution when it presents itself. He bounces back when he's hurt.

Finally, a good potential president is able to handle multiple pressures. The president of a large dry cleaning and laundry company in New York puts it this way: "Anyone can do a good job if you give him one problem at a time and all the time he needs to solve it. But when I see a man unwilling to pay attention to anything else until he gets his one little problem solved, I worry. That kind of man never knows there's a fire next door until the whole company burns down."

#5. HOW DO I HANDLE AN EXECUTIVE WHO OVERRATES
     HIMSELF FOR PROMOTION?

Be certain of your groundwork. How certain are you that he's not ready? Could it be that you don't recognize the work and effort that has earned him a promotion?

Of course, if he is not doing a good job in his present position, forget it. This guy is going nowhere. He probably feels, "Well, I'm no good in the engine room but if I could only be the captain of the ship, it would be easier." The guy who thinks he is too big for his present assignment, who thinks he'd be great if only he were president or general manager, he is your worst trap. If he's down on quota, has a high turnover rate, or his people think he's too aggressive, he doesn't even belong in the company, let alone be under consideration for a promotion.

The more I encounter this sort of situation, and I see it all the time, the more I am convinced that managers have a wonderful tool at hand which they rarely use—evidence: production standards met or not met, quotas made or not made, profit and loss, personnel turnover, and so forth. Aldous Huxley said, "The facts do not cease to exist because they are ignored." Don't play the hunches, neither your own nor his. Don't promote on the *possibility* that this man may suddenly take off like a rocket. If he hasn't done a good job in the past, then you're wasting your time. Though your job is to develop people, you can't develop potential if this guy hasn't proved to you that he has some. One executive said to me, "It's like trying to grow grass on concrete. If it's not there, it's not there. You have to give me something to grow it on."

That's why initial selection is so important. You can make a good man turn sour by treating him poorly, by not giving him sufficient opportunity, but you can't take a benchwarmer and make him a star. You don't have the time, the resources, the ability, or the environment to change what was fundamentally given to a man early in life, in childhood.

What do I tell this man who is not ready for promotion, but who is constantly pressuring me for the bigger job?

Tell him the truth, gently. The hardest thing to do is to take a man who is 35 years old and say to him, "In my opinion, you don't have what it takes for management. You can make the decision, to stay or to leave. But if you stay, you will remain at about the same level. My present estimate is that you will not progress much further, and, with the exception of small salary increments, you aren't going up. I am the boss. But, where there's death, there's hope. With your next boss, maybe you will do a little better. But that's my present reading."

The president of a life insurance company told me recently that this is his *most* difficult task. "I end careers when I do this. I have led men crying from my office. But I know I'm doing the right thing," he said, "not only for the company, but also for the men I've counseled. One man left our company and became a violin teacher. Now he teaches music in the high school and he's a great violinist. He's very happy, too. I'm pleased that I counseled him early enough to help him change his pattern of life. *He would have made a lousy manager.*"

#6. HOW CAN I HOLD ON TO AN AMBITIOUS SUBORDINATE, ONE FOR WHOM I DON'T HAVE A PROMOTION SPOT AT THE MOMENT?

Give him special projects. Send him to conventions. Give him speaking assignments. Let him explore some areas of the company that you think could stand some objective appraisal. Make him a trouble-shooter. Tell him to go to Denver and investigate that nagging problem you've had for six months, then come back and write a report, give you his ideas.

There are a multitude of ways to keep ambitious men happy. One president does this: Whenever he goes on a trip, he'll pick one or two of his key executives and take them with him. These are top men whom he can't really promote at the moment. There just aren't any openings.

He takes these men in the company plane. It gives him a chance to talk with them, to get some of their ideas, and to give them the impression that they are on the move. What's more, they get the feeling that they would be foolish to leave the firm, because they're getting closer and closer to the president.

The problem you have to avoid here is that the senior man—the fellow who may be directly in line and who is blocking the path of promotion—gets upset. But this is the risk you run. You have to talk to the senior man. Tell him, "Listen, we all have a stake in this. Unless we can make people, we're not going to make any more money. We have to guarantee an income of people to guarantee our financial income tomorrow, next year and after we retire. This is one way I'm building people. I'm giving them increased exposure."

#7. HOW CAN I INSPIRE A GOOD MAN WHO LACKS CONFIDENCE IN HIMSELF?

A straight frontal attack—"Come on, boy, pull yourself together. Stop going around here like a mollycoddle. Be more assertive."—won't work. This guy will say, "Yeah, my wife tells me the same thing." He may be more confident for a week or so, but then he's worse than before.

First, make sure that this man is capable. Then, *assuming he is a man of ability,* approach him on this basis:

"Look, I'm not going to tell you to be more self-confident. That's ridiculous. But let's see what the psychologists say about this. I've done some reading, and I have some information that might help you.

"Try to accept your own limitations. You will never be as great as you could wish. Somerset Maugham said, in his autobiography *Summing Up*, 'I knew that I had no lyrical quality, a small vocabulary, little gift of metaphor. The original and striking simile never occurred to me. Poetic flights . . . were beyond my powers. On the other hand, I had an acute power of observation, and it seemed to me that I could see a great many things that other people missed. I could put down in clear terms what I saw . . . I knew that I should never write as well as I could wish, but I thought, with pains, that I could arrive at writing as well as my natural defects allowed.'

"Also, respect your own functioning. Say, 'These are the jobs I can do well, and the past has demonstrated this to be true.' The problem may be that you haven't communicated this effectively to other people. Do you loosen up at a party? Do you communicate effectively socially? Why at home and not in the office?

"Finally, I want you to analyze yourself. You gain self-confidence by self-analysis, and by setting your goals slightly above what you *know* you can achieve. Not too much above, because then you are doomed to failure, but slightly above."

With some people, it helps to remind them that everyone has strengths and weaknesses, and that the differences in life are not big, tremendous differences, but slight edges. If you're a good hitter, one-quarter of an inch up or down on the bat makes a big difference in your average. Tell him to maximize *his* slight edge by taking advantage of it, and to forget altogether those deficiencies which he will never be able to correct no matter how much effort he puts out.

Suppose he's weak in decision-making? He delays, stalls, can't make the critical choice. Even when he makes the decision, has no confidence in it? What do I tell him?

You motivate him with encouragement. With people like this it sometimes works. Here's the kind of thing you tell him:

"Look, you're going to be on this team. As long as I'm the manager, you're going to play center field and no one else is going to take your job away. I think you're capable. Now, unless you believe that yourself, deep down, I can't help you. You've got to work on your inside image, and you're going to have to practice self-confidence at home, in church, in the office, with your kids and everyone else you meet.

"Also, don't communicate your fears; keep them to yourself. When Truman decided to use the first atom bomb, he didn't go to the public and say, 'I'm not quite sure that this is the right thing to do.' He knew this would have destroyed the public's confidence in him."

This man of yours who is weak in decision-making, he thinks that some people are decisive and some are indecisive. He believes the ones who are indecisive are that way because they have all these fears, and that the confident guys have no doubts. That's untrue. The confident guy is just as loaded with fear as everyone else, but he doesn't let others know about it. He doesn't ventilate his anxieties.

Can I trust him to make important decisions during his period of building self-confidence? Would this help him?

Yes. Give him a test. Tell him to keep a diary of his decisions, and ask him to report back to you in a month, or six months, with the results. You don't want to know about the decisions until the results are in. At the end of the waiting period, review each decision with him and see how he came out. If he did well, he'll gain confidence. But if he did do poorly, you'll have to clobber him and look for another man. You can't keep reassuring him forever when he's wrong. If he doesn't gain confidence, nothing else you can do will help. He needs psychiatric help because his lack of confidence comes not from reality, but from something which you know nothing about.

#8. HOW CAN I MAKE A TOUGH JOB MORE APPEALING?
   WHAT INCENTIVES CAN I USE?

Managers have a great tendency to make promises in order to seduce a man into taking on more responsibility. When you want to talk a good man into taking on a tough job, don't promise him anything, and *don't say anything which he will construe as a promise*. For example, you may say in an offhanded manner, "You know, this job means a lot. Properly handled, it could earn you a shot at the vice-presidency." So this guy goes back to his office and says, "Oh, boy. I'm gonna be vice-president. The boss just told me so." And he goes home and tells his wife and the next thing you know, everybody in the firm—except you—knows who the next vice-president is going to be.

But you have to make him believe that the job is terribly important. Here's how to do it without promising:

Avoid situations where you might be saddled with the reputation of being a phony, a manager who makes promises he won't keep. Avoid mentioning the future and you'll be safe. Don't talk about where this guy may be in six months, or six years, because this carries implications of a guarantee you may not be able to keep.

But the guy presses you: "Why are you giving me this job? Can you promise me a reward?" Tell him this: "Look, here's the job I want done. Here is where we are now; but we are moving, and we both know that it isn't always going to be like this. I cannot promise you what will be, because I cannot control the future. I might *tell* you that I will make you a top manager but I can't guarantee it, and I don't want you to get worked up over *possibilities*. I know too much about life to make promises I may not be able to keep. I don't want to doom you to disappointment.

"Where is the promise? It is within you and within your capacity to deliver. Peter Drucker, author and management consultant, said, 'Regarding the future, there are no certainties, only expectations.' No one can guarantee you a future, only an opportunity for you to develop your own future."

I have a problem with executive job applicants who insist on knowing about the future. How can I hire them without making promises?

If the applicant seems reluctant to take on the position without a promise of promotion or success, then you're being manipulated. You're in a trap. If you have to promise him the future, you're talking to the wrong man. He won't be realistic about the present. He's dreaming about the future. He's pushing you and you've been oversold. Admit it.

9. HOW CAN I HANDLE A SENSITIVE EXECUTIVE WHO NEEDS
IMPROVEMENT IN HIS PERSONAL APPEARANCE?

This is relatively easy. I find that people accept criticism of
material things easier than they'll accept criticism of their perso-
nalities.

One of the best ways to handle the problem is through the
process of what we psychologists call "identification." If your
executive can identify himself with you—by being seen with you,
by doing the things you do, by wearing the kind of clothes you
wear—he can lift his sights and change his self-image and the
image he presents to associates and subordinates.

Approach the problem directly. Tell him, "Look, if it's a financial
problem—I'm aware that you have trouble making ends meet
because of repairs to the house and the kids are sick—if it's money,
let me give you a hand." Buy him a suit occasionally, or get him
a gift certificate at a leading store. Send him to your tailor. He
can be just as creative and as dynamic in a nice business suit as
he can in argyle socks and a shabby sports jacket.

Tell him, "If you look sloppy, you'll probably feel sloppy. If
you dress neatly, you'll feel better and probably do better work.
Women know this. When they're depressed, they go out and buy
a new hat. Hayakawa said that a new hat may look terrible on
a woman, but it looks great on her self-image. I have an image of
you. So has everyone else. Now, the higher up you move in the
company's ranks, the more important this image becomes. If you
are to be exposed as an officer of this firm to our clients, executives
in other companies, and the public, then you must look as if you
have the trappings of command."

This fellow may be caught up in a social circle of friends who
dress, speak, or behave in a manner which is unacceptable in the
executive suite. If so, say, "Look, I don't expect you to abandon
your old friends. This is your private matter. But I don't think
that these friends are helping you much in terms of the people
you will have to meet and deal with as an executive in this company. Broaden your outlook. Get involved in the Rotary, civic
affairs and other areas in which you will make new friends. In
fact, I'm going to take you to some of my own meetings, where
your only purpose will be to meet people and sit there and

observe." Ask him to sit in on top-level conferences, to have lunch with your executive group. He'll learn quickly.

10. HOW CAN I TELL A LOYAL EMPLOYEE THAT HE HAS BEEN PASSED OVER FOR PROMOTION?

I know of no easy way.

If he is an older man, be sincere. Say, "Frank, I made the decision. I'm sorry you didn't get the job. I know this may be the last opportunity you'll have for that job. But I'm the boss, and I had to make a tough decision."

If he doesn't ask "Why?" you're home safe. He's let you off the hook. If he asks for the reasons why, try once more to put him off: "A combination of reasons led me to make the decision, and I'm not at liberty to reveal them. I have been asked to operate in confidence, and you just have to accept that there's nothing either of us can do about it."

But if he still comes back and says, "You owe it to me to let me know. Why?" Then give him the reasons: You need a salesman as manager and he's an engineer; you need a man in the East, and he has established himself in Chicago; you need a man who will do a lot of traveling, and he's basically an internal operative.

If he is a younger man, take a different approach: "There are ample opportunities ahead. But the future rests with you. This time you didn't quite measure up. You have been too impulsive, you overlook details occasionally, you've let the rest of us down from time to time, you haven't followed up. And as long as you continue this behavior it's going to be difficult to promote you. But I think you have potential. Your general performance indicates this is so. You missed one chance, but there will be others.

"George Bernard Shaw said, 'My tailor is the only man who understands me. He takes my measurements every time we meet.' All I can tell you, Joe, is that I will continue to take your measurements, and if you show a change, I will be open-minded about your next promotion opportunity."

Of course, if you feel that there is absolutely no chance that this man will change or grow, then you should tell him so.

In either case, be he older or younger, the man who is passed over should be removed from any intimate contact with the man who was promoted. It will also help if you minimize the number of contacts that *you* have with him. His hurt will heal in time, but if you se him too often, you may re-open the wound before it is even sutured. Get him away, at least for a while.

Naturally, you take a chance on losing him. The older he is, the less likely; the younger, the more likely. The less driven, the less likely; the more ambitious, the more likely. You're taking a calculated risk.

Don't overlook the possibility that he will be so upset and angry about being passed over, he may start a campaign against you. He might start digging holes for you to fall into. When that happens, get rid of him. He's a bad apple. You haven't got the time to worry about him.

2.

Be Objective About
Your Managerial Ability

This chapter will take you on a journey into what, for most executives, is a foreign land. It will not be an easy journey, because one of the hardest things a man can do is to look at himself objectively and realistically, without self-glorification, deception, or despair.

As Dr. Arnold J. Toynbee, the philosophic historian, once said, "No human beings have got very far in the exploration of the spiritual universe. The new worlds with whose life it is now most urgent for us to make contact are the spiritual worlds within ourselves."

A self-analysis can pay rich dividends in at least three ways:

1. Increased managerial effectiveness and impact on others.
2. Better personal relationships.
3. Greater personal fulfillment.

"Only as you know yourself," says Bernard M. Baruch, "can your brain serve you as a sharp and efficient tool. Know your own failings, passions, and prejudices so you can separate them from what you see." (This is a serious problem for most people. They daydream of spectacular achievements far into the future, making the day-to-day improvements seem of little importance. But without the small, continuous, day-to-day improvements, the spectacular achievements of the future will *never* be reached.)

The human being has come a long way in the direction of self-understanding, though he still has much to learn. By comparison with his primitive ancestors, he knows a great deal; stone-age tribesmen in Australia still cannot associate their headaches with their own heads. Even in that physical sense, they are strangers to themselves.

The modern manager is not only aware of his headaches, he has advanced to a familiar knowledge of his ulcers, pulse, and blood pressure!

But you need to know yourself other than in the language of your ills and aches. All too often, self-study takes place only in times of crisis, when you get a distorted picture of your strengths and deficiencies. For a balanced picture, you have to look at yourself in relatively normal situations and stable circumstances.

The task is not easy. The psychoanalyst Dr. Ada Hirsh, in writing on the possibilities of self-analysis, pointed out the need for the following prerequisites:

A substantial degree of psychological health.
A desire to come closer to the truth about ourselves.
A belief in the ability to change.
An ability to think logically with an open mind and courage.

Why you avoid seeing yourself as others do

"Getting to know you," according to a popular song, *seems* to be a simple matter of learning a little bit day by day. It is not quite that simple. Every man builds up a strong network of defenses which act to protect him from others and, incidentally, from himself.

Everyone is born into this world helpless and dependent. In order to survive, everyone needs to lean on others. The child growing up learns to turn to mother not only for the physical comforts but also for the more rewarding comfort of approval.

As a man grows older, he continues the search for approval from the widening circle around him. He wants friends not only to like him but to approve of what he does. In their approval he finds reassurance of his own worth.

So great is the human need for love and approval that a man will even deceive himself, if necessary, rather than face the fact that he might not deserve it. Undisguised, his behavior might not always merit approval. He may do things that are inconsiderable, unkind, or even downright cruel. But rather than face himself in an unkind light, even to his own eyes, his unconscious mind will protect his image of himself. Thus:

1. He rationalizes. He says, "I did it because . . . ," providing good and substantial reasons for his behavior.
2. He projects. He disowns the fault, seeing it as the other fellow's problem.
3. He displaces. He blames someone else for his own faults that he cannot accept.
4. He compensates. He stretches himself in one area when he has failed in another.

A classic illustration of rationalization is told by a vice-president, a former alcoholic. He expressed the way his mind deceived him as follows:

> When I was young and just out of college I found the nicest people in bars. The men were bright and the women charming. Soon, I got into the habit of heading to the bar about four in the afternoon and staying there 'till two in the morning.
>
> But as I got older, it seemed that the crowd was deteriorating! The most charming people never showed anymore.
>
> Rather than believe I was becoming an alcoholic, I figured it all out another way. The bartenders were responsible. They weren't as intelligent as they used to be when I was younger.
>
> I therefore set about to correct the situation by spending time moving from bar to bar, giving the whiskey tenders tests of general information. I felt certain that if bartenders were more interesting and informed, then all the best people would return!

This man developed an elaborate and "reasonable" explanation for his growing need for alcohol. His rationalization was his attempt at self-deception.

The confederate leader Jefferson Davis is another example. Davis, a graduate of the U. S. Military Academy, resigned from the Army in 1835 to become a planter and prosperous slaveholder. Then he was elected to Congress and became a public figure. But in 1846, after more than 10 years of military retirement, he enlisted in the First Mississippi Infantry to fight in the Mexican War. He was given the rank of colonel and served with distinction at Buena Vista and Monterrey in 1846-47. Later he was elected provisional president of the Confederacy.

During the Civil War, Davis won notoriety for foolishly directing the movements of his generals. His interference with his generals was frequent and often disastrous. Historians say that his faulty military logic was one of the basic causes of the South's tragedy.

Why did Davis interfere? He confused fantasy with reality. He believed that his was one of the outstanding military minds of his day. He believed that his voluntary retirement and his comeback successes during the Mexican War proved his military logic to be sound. That was fantasy. Realistically, Davis' military mind was weak; only *he* believed it to be strong. Actually, his generals might have been able to wage a far superior war without his "help."

A man's defenses, then, serve two purposes, neither of which is particularly valid. First, they represent an attempt to prove to others that he really is a fine person, and anything he does wrong is done for the right reason. Secondly, and probably more important, they help the man to deceive himself. They help him to retain the image of himself as an important and productive gentleman. While the alcoholic is an extreme case, the wall of defense is so solid in most men that it becomes a barrier to self-knowledge.

Your unconscious prevents you from succeeding

The road to self-knowledge is further blocked by the unconscious mind, which exerts much control over behavior. Dr. Sigmund Freud, the father of modern psychoanalysis, was the first

to understand the importance of the unconscious in deterl
behavior.

The real problem emerges because safety devices operating
from the unconscious work automatically. You have to be very
skillful if you want to sneak up on yourself and take a quick look.
How many times have you found yourself doing the opposite of
what you consciously intended to do?

Dr. William Menninger of the famed clinic says, "This sort of
thing is most vividly seen in people who can't stop eating. They
will make all kinds of resolutions about going on a diet; but they
seem powerless to stick to their decisions. Obviously, some unconscious pressure is forcing them to go on doing the things
that, consciously, they want to stop doing."

Most executives at some time or other have had the same sort
of trouble getting a particular chore done. You promise yourself
that you will get to it at the very first opportunity, but you never
seem able to find the time.

Dr. Burleigh B. Gardner, a respected social anthropologist,
points out some of the reasons why managers delay or fail in
spite of their conscious desire to succeed:

1. *Desire to be something else.* Often many capable people
don't like supervisory work and resent the demands it makes on
them.

2. *Unconscious desire to be someone else.* Many men have the
ambition characteristic of good managers. "Often, however, the
desire for a supervisory position is merely a means to some other
end and a man has no interest in the work for its own satisfactions."

3. *Inability to make room for others.* Many men, in spite of
their conscious desire to cooperate with others, just can't seem to
make the grade. They resent the advancement of anyone else.
Although these men may provide you with reasons, they often are
unaware of the fact that underneath their inability to work co-
operatively lies a deep resentment toward others.

4. *Resistance to authority.* Psychologists point out that resistance to authority takes many disguised forms, such as chronic
lateness, forgetting important meetings and messages for a

ng special privileges and ignoring directions.
ho resorts to these tactics may be unaware of
is striking out against his superiors because he
is almost as if the person is saying, "I know you
I'll reject you before you have a chance to reject me."

Sometimes, then, a man may be unaware of the fact that he is blocking his own path. As playwright Ben Hecht observes:

> A wise man knows that he has only one enemy—himself. This is an enemy difficult to ignore and full of cunning. It assails one with doubts and fear. It always seeks to loosen and lead one away from one's goal. It is an enemy never to be forgotten but constantly outwitted.

Find out the truth about yourself

The quest for self-knowledge is as old as Adam and Eve. Yet, man still knows very little about himself. Most people are totally unaware of their own feelings, emotions, beliefs, and goals.

Professor Werner Wolff of Bard College once conducted a simple experiment that dramatizes man's unfamiliarity with himself. He asked people to identify themselves and their friends in a set of pictures in which the faces were hidden. The average person had trouble picking himself out of a crowd; he had better luck labeling the pictures of his acquaintances!

If you have ever seen home movies of yourself or listened to a recording of your voice, you have probably said to yourself, "Is that me?" If you have been astonished by the unfamiliarity with your *outer* shell—your appearance and voice—imagine how much *more* difficult it is to get to know about your inner self.

Yet, in spite of difficulties, the search for self-knowledge is critical to your role as an industrial leader. Where do you start? One way might be to face up to some searching questions.

	Yes	No
1. Do you ever find yourself agreeing to something contrary to your real beliefs?	☐	☐
2. Have you ever had a nonsensical dream?	☐	☐

3. Have you ever been in an unaccountable mood that you couldn't shake? ☐ ☐

4. Did you ever feel really wonderful about something from the past that made little impact when it occurred? ☐ ☐

5. Have you ever been surprised at the reactions of others to what you say or do? ☐ ☐

6. Have you ever been embarrassed by a slip of the tongue? ☐ ☐

7. Have you ever found yourself repeating a confidence you had vowed never to reveal? ☐ ☐

8. Are you often disappointed in other people or surprised that they turn out better than you thought?

9. Have you ever cried at a movie that you later considered sloppy and sentimental? ☐ ☐

10. Do you think you know where you want to be five years from today? Ten years from today? ☐ ☐

Dr. Schuyler Hoslett, former vice-president of Dun & Bradstreet, now Dean of Business Administration at the University of Hawaii, has another brief but probing list of questions that often helps in the search for self-understanding. He suggests that the executive think through the answers to the following four questions whenever he is restless or dissatisfied:

1. What am I here for? What is the purpose of life for me?

2. Why do I work with this organization? Does it fit my purpose in life?

3. What can this organization do to help me fulfill my meaning in the world? Has it helped me so far to fulfill my purpose?

4. Assuming that I choose to remain in this organization, how can I help to fulfill my meaning and my purpose in the world?

Neither list of questions can be adequately answered on the spot. In fact, the quicker and easier the answers come, the less you should trust them. Deceptively simple in appearance, each one deserves serious probing and careful thought. Uncovering the truth about yourself may yield a few surprises—but you'll be the richer for the digging.

Five techniques for studying yourself

The professional techniques for studying personality are very complicated. To penetrate to real depth, you may have to call in the expert. But many of the instruments used by the psychologist to probe into character can be adapted for use by the average executive. For a deeper search of self, you might try one or more of the five methods outlined below. Not all of them are suitable for everyone. Read the descriptions and choose the method that you feel you can apply most successfully.

1. THE AUTOBIOGRAPHICAL APPROACH

Some people may find it fruitful to probe the past, to uncover the critical incidents that helped determine what they are today. This can be done fairly easily, starting out with your earliest memories about the important people in your life.

● What was your father like? How did you react to him as a person? Did you resent his discipline then, and did you later come to understand his motives? What hopes did he have for you? What dreams did you dream together about the future? Do you find yourself acting in some ways toward your children as he did toward you?

● And what about your mother? What kind of person was she? How did you get along? Were you her favorite child?

● How about your teachers and other school authorities? What were your reactions to them?

Be honest in your answers. All children have conflicts with their parents and other adults. Mature people can recognize the nature of the conflicts and understand now what they might not have understood then. If you have this understanding, you are less likely to continue to act out your childhood conflicts in adult life. We sometimes bet on horses that have already run their races.

Reactions to all kinds of authority are often a continuation of the relationship you had with your parents. A study of your past can help you better handle the present and, most important, it can aid in building a better foundation for the future. Other key questions you might ask yourself include:

- What successes in school made me proudest?
- What were the disappointments in my life?
- What kind of people are my friends?
- Which experiences give me the most satisfaction?

But don't look just for dramatic and easily recalled memories from your past. These may be important, but they are apt to give you a distorted picture. Take a look at the small details that stay with you, that recur whenever you think about the past. These undoubtedly played a part in shaping you.

2. NOTE THE EXTREMES

Your highs and lows, the extremes of your emotions and feelings, often provide a clue to the core which lies hidden in your everyday behavior. The unusual is, in effect, an exaggeration of the usual.

Too often, a busy man is prone to dismiss unusual behavior as not typical. "That's not like me," he says, and discounts it completely. But an analysis of the times he got angrier than he supposed was possible, reveals more truthfully his "normal" behavior.

Try this experiment for a week. Keep a diary of your reactions and the situations which caused them. They might be just fleeting moments of feeling: exhilaration, anger, frustration. Or they might be lifts of spirit that last all day. This does not matter. What counts is that your behavior be stronger than usual, and that you experienced it. Here are the steps that will help you examine these events and uncover their significance:

- *Record the situation and the reaction.* Jot down the feelings and as much of the details of their causes as you can possibly capture. Be certain that you record enough information to bring it all back to mind later

- *Accumulate a variety.* It is best to accumulate at least five different types of situations before you examine and review them.

If a week does not provide enough time, take 10 days or two weeks; but make sure you have several items in your diary.

● *Analyze them.* When you have recorded enough separate items to form a picture, look at them in relation to each other. Is there any common thread or pattern? Is there a special time of the day, a particular individual, a problem or situation which appears repeatedly? What is your role in each situation? Are you the bystander or an active participant? What did you contribute to the good situations? What about the bad ones? Do you think that you can predict your behavior better now than you could before?

● *Reverse roles.* Review those events that involved other people, playing them in your mind like a movie. But make this big difference—change your role. Try to picture yourself in the role of the other person. See if the story unfolds in the same way. Would you now make the other person angry, or happy, as he made you feel in the original scene? You'll learn much about yourself by trying to fit yourself into the shoes of people to whom you react strongly.

3. ANALYSIS OF DREAMS

"Dreams which are not interpreted are like letters which have not been opened," says the Talmud. Dreams are messages from yourself to yourself, and they constitute one of the most important sources leading to self-knowledge. Psychologists find in dreams a royal road to an understanding of their patients.

However, in spite of their rich source of insight, dreams are best left to the experts. Dr. Erich Fromm, the noted psychologist, has pointed out some of the reasons why dreams are so difficult for the average individual to interpret:

● *Different rules of logic apply.* Dreams appear nonsensical sometimes, because they are not bound by the logic of waking life. For example, you may dream that a man you know turned into a chicken. In realistic terms this is silly. But if you think he is a coward, it makes sense to your emotions and feelings. These are the things that matter in dreams, not the realities of everyday living.

● *Time doesn't matter.* Events that happened in your childhood may be transplanted into the present.

● *Relative importance of things may be distorted.* A comparatively small annoyance with another person may give rise to a dream that the other man fell sick and thus is now incapable of annoying you. Yet, you might not really be that angry with him.

To discover the importance of a wish expressed in a dream, you must look further. If a theme is repeated night after night, if your reaction to the dream is accompanied by unusual distress, if you resist unravelling the dream — all these are indications of a strong hidden feeling.

There are times when dreams can provide you with flashes of insight. For example, your judgments about people may be more astute when you are dreaming. You are not influenced by general opinion or by what you think is the right way to feel. Further, dreams may provide clues to important events that you did not consider significant when they occurred. Dr. Fromm points out that dreams may show that an occurrence thought to be insignificant actually was important and may even indicate what its importance consisted of!

Dr. Calvin Hall, who has analyzed more than 10,000 dreams, summarizes his impressions in the following way. During sleep we think about our problems and predicaments, our fears and hopes. The dreamer thinks about himself: What kind of person he is, and how well fitted he is to deal with his conflicts and anxieties. He thinks about other people who touch his life intimately. We see how he looks to himself, how others look to him, and how he conceives of life. This is the heart of the matter and the reason why dreams are important data for the psychologist.

How a person sees himself is expressed in dreams by the parts the dreamer plays. He may play the part of a victim or an aggressor or both; he may conceive of himself as winning in spite of adverse circumstances, or losing because of these same adversities. He may assume the role of a saint or a sinner, a dependent person or an independent one, a miser or a philanthropist. However, it takes sensitivity and skill to read your own dreams and uncover these meanings.

4. CHANGE OF ROUTINE

Most people tend to become blind to the familiar and accustomed things around them. Until a visit from a stranger jolts you into looking at your surroundings through new eyes, you may remain unaware of the most obvious facts.

More important, you may lose yourself in the rush of daily pressures, becoming insensitive to your own reactions.

Anne Morrow Lindbergh felt this need to get away from daily pressures — the running of a home, the endless committee meetings, the demands of her five children. To rediscover herself, she decided to break the pattern of routine. So she took a few weeks at the beach in new surroundings. Her beautiful, sensitive book *Gift from the Sea* describes some of the discoveries she made about herself during this period.

Even if you can't take a few weeks at the shore, you can accomplish the same goal in other ways:

● Go through an entire day as if you were about to leave the job or the community. How would you act? What would you notice if you felt that you would never be here again?

● Pretend that you had to explain all of your actions and decisions to a child. Go through a day imagining the questions a 12-year-old might ask about your work habits.

● Spend a day alone, with no fixed program. If possible, and if the family will understand, take a solo trip in your car, letting your mood determine your destination.

● Examine new by-ways. Take a new route even if it's only on the way to work.

● Take a trip back to your old home town and search out remembered landmarks.

● Spend a day pretending that you and one of your subordinates have switched roles. Try to act as he would.

By changing your point of view for a day, you can often open your eyes and see yourself and your behavior in a new light. The more frequently you get out of your rut and look around, the more freshness and insight you gain.

5. CROSS-CHARACTERIZATION

In his book *My Autobiography*, Charlie Chaplin told an interesting anecdote that illustrates the principle of cross-characterization and its important role in self-discovery. Chaplin was at a party in London attended by many distinguished guests, among them the Prince of Wales:

> Someone that evening introduced a game that was prevalent in America, called "Frank Estimations." The guests were each given a card with ten qualifications on it: charm, intelligence, personality, sex appeal, good looks, sincerity, sense of humor, adaptability, and so forth. A guest left the room and marked up his card with a frank estimation of his own qualifications, giving himself from one to the maximum of ten—for instance, I gave myself seven for a sense of humor, six for sex appeal, six for good looks, eight for adaptability, four for sincerity. Meanwhile, each guest gave an appraisal of the victim who had left the room, marking his card secretly. Then the victim entered and read off the marks he had given himself, and a spokesman read aloud the cards of the guests to see how they tallied.
>
> When the Prince's turn came he announced three for sex appeal, the guests averaged him four, I gave him five; some cards read only two. For good looks, the Prince gave himself six, the guests averaged him eight, and I marked him seven. For charm he announced five, the guests gave him eight, and I gave him eight. For sincerity the Prince announced the limit, ten, the guests averaged him three and a half, I gave him four. The Prince was indignant. "Sincerity is the most important qualification I think I have," he said.

Remember Poet John Masefield's lines:

> And there were three men
> Went down the road as down the road went he:
> The man they saw, the man he was,
>   the man he wanted to be.

To unify all three and make them one person is among the chief targets of life. But to achieve it, you must first reconcile the person *they see* with the person *you are*. Reprinted below is a list of personal descriptions adapted from a Richardson, Bellows, Henry & Co. test for self-evaluation. Read over the list and add any other descriptions that especially apply to you; then proceed as follows:

In the first column, "Self," put a check next to every adjective that you feel applies to you. Check as many as appropriate. Under "Superior," check the words you think your superiors would consider appropriate for you. Under "Wife," put your best guess of your wife's estimate. Repeat the same process under "Friend." Then add up all the checks for a summary verdict.

	Self	Superior	Wife	Friend	Verdict
Kind					
Truthful					
Argumentative					
Eager					
Tense					
Generous					
Humble					
Firm					
Optimistic					
Egotistic					
Shrewd					
Good mixer					
Selfish					
Easily swayed					
Impulsive					
Talkative					
Confident					
Willing					
Touchy					
Sentimental					
Grouchy					
Aggressive					
Slow					
Reliable					

Aloof
Efficient
Tactful
Fair
Hostile
Observant
Stubborn
Hothead
Dreamer

Now, to interpret your responses, here are some guides. First, look at the "Self" column. Good and Bad should be evenly divided. If there are too many negatives or if you rarely checked the strongly favorable characteristics, then you may not be looking at yourself with sufficient objectivity.

The number of items checked is a measure of your personal complexity. "The more items you believe are characteristic," points out Dr. Harold Musaker, "the more elaborate your self-portrait."

The comparison between the answers you marked for yourself and those characteristics you believe others would attribute to you provide another key to self-understanding. There should be some difference. We all play more than one role. Obviously, people see you from different vantage points. One friend will see one aspect of you; your wife another; your superior another. It is appropriate that we show different faces under different circumstances. The real understanding comes in when you are able to interpret why others see you differently.

There should be a basic personality core emerging, about which you and others agree. If there's too great a difference in the profile that emerges from column to column, then you'd better sit down and try to decide which one comes closest to the truth. Are you looking at yourself through tinted glasses? You may be better than others think, or you may not be revealing the same face to different people, or you may be misunderstanding what they think of you.

The real challenge is in your willingness to weigh the answers and distill the truth. Why would someone else think you are timid, or courageous, or persuasive? Why should a friend think one thing, your superior another, when you possibly disagree with both? Perhaps you will never come up with a final answer, but the effort will teach you many things about yourself, helping you to project the image you want to project.

Charting the future

Jack Nail, District Sales Manager of Du Pont, once remarked after he gave his men a self-evaluation chart, "I didn't give my men a tough assignment. I gave 'em an impossible one."

To recognize the difficulties of self-study, it might be helpful in summary to highlight some guidelines:

1. AVOID USING SELF-STUDY FOR SELF-PUNISHMENT

As an executive, you undoubtedly have many positive traits which helped you arrive at your present position. Most executives have faced and conquered the challenges of marriage, children, and work. Nothing is gained by trying to pick yourself apart, interpreting minor weaknesses as major failures.

2. RECOGNIZE THE PROBLEMS INVOLVED

Dr. Karen Horney points out in her book on self-analysis:

> People who embark on that promised easy road will either acquire a false smugness, believing they know all about themselves, or will become discouraged when they are blocked by the first serious obstacle and will tend to relinquish the search for truth as a bad job. Neither result will happen so easily if one is aware that self-analysis is a strenuous, slow process, bound to be painful and upsetting at times and requiring all available constructive energies.

3. EXPECT SMALL CHANGES, SETTLE FOR SLOW PROGRESS

Decide on just one or two areas for improvement. Don't try to change yourself completely. Remember, no one destroys a house because there may be a few leaks in the roof. Here are specific areas that executives might consider as targets for change:

Learn to disagree without being offensive.
Learn to stop needling.
Learn how to draw people out.

Learn to be forceful without being domineering.
Learn how to avoid passing your own anxiety on to subordinates
Learn how to be less impulsive.

4. RECOGNIZE WHY YOU WANT TO CHANGE

If others claim that you don't listen to them, then you must see clearly why better listening will help you. Otherwise you'll have little incentive to change your behavior. However, if others accuse you of being too aggressive, you might decide that drive is an essential aspect of your personality and a key to success. Thus, you may dismiss this complaint as "their problem." You can't change yourself to suit everyone. But you do owe it to yourself to weigh their reactions objectively, to understand the reasons for your own behavior, and then to choose the course you wish to follow.

5. DECIDE ON THE PROPER BALANCE

Every negative has its positive. The basic question, according to Dr. Richard Wallin, an industrial psychologist, is "What could I do to retain the advantages while giving up the disadvantages?" If we unconsciously alienate people in order to keep them from making demands upon us, could we prevent the demands without alienating the people? Or, as in the previous illustration, could we salvage the drive without antagonizing others by our aggressiveness?

6. DIFFERENTIATE THE LONG RANGE PERSONAL GOALS FROM THE SHORT RANGE IMMEDIATE ONES

Joe Crail, president of Coast Federal Savings and Loan Association in Los Angeles, outlines short range goals as follows: learning a little more about my job; making small improvements in performance; analyzing current activities and methods for improvement. These areas are immediate and 75 per cent capable of achievement. The long range goals are vague and indefinite — like making lots of money, gaining prestige, becoming president, retirement, freedom from demands, etc. The problem may be that you dream of making changes to achieve long range goals, which depletes the mental energy you need to make yourself a little better for the short range goals of today.

In the final analysis, you must recognize that there are flaws in your personality which you must accept with simple resignation. Self-study can be valuable in attempting change, even if it does nothing more than help you to decide which traits *cannot* be changed!

3.

Controlling and Using
Your Executive Drive

There's nothing like drive. It can mean everything.

One of the classic displays is attributed to John T. Connor, Secretary of Commerce and former president of Merck & Co.

When Connor was 40 years old and just another executive with Merck, the retiring president Dr. Vannevar Bush began looking around for a successor. Bush asked among his 30 top executives as to their choice for a new president. Most of them named Connor. People knew him as a driven man with a strong ego.

When Connor himself was asked he said, "I should be the new president."

Connor got the job. He got it largely because he has what he himself believes most successful businessmen must have: a Cassius Clay syndrome - "I am the greatest." Connor rose to the top because he knew he could handle the presidency better than anyone else.

What does it take to make a man like Connor tick? What are the factors that underlie your own drive for success? For many

years psychologists believed that the basic physiological drives
—hunger, thirst, and sex—constituted our basic motivational
factors and influenced all our actions. Thus it was assumed that
the drive to succeed was similarly based on the need to satisfy
these conditions. The ways in which any individual satisfied
these needs were merely determined by the culture in which
he lived, observers believed.

The drive to be more competent

However, recent research by some eminent psychologists indicates that man has still another basic need to which attention
has not hitherto been paid. This need was first examined in
depth about two or three years ago by Dr. Robert White at Harvard, who calls it the need to exercise *competence*.

White claims that this is one of the prime motivators of individuals. It is so dominant, he says, that it even occurs in lower
orders of animals. The desire for competence promotes the need
for activity and exploration, and the need to deal effectively
with the environment. "Years of research," says White, "have
pretty much destroyed the orthodox drive model (hunger, thirst,
and sex). It is no longer appropriate to consider that drives or-
iginate solely in tissue deficits external to the nervous system,
that consummatory acts are a universal feature and goal of motivated behavior, or that the alleviation of tissue deficits is the
necessary condition for instrumental learning."

Industrial psychologists observing and studying executive behavior, are especially persuaded by Dr. White's theories. I find
that men, particularly business executives who have it within
their power to make or break others as well as themselves, are
driven by the need for self-satisfaction, for competence — indeed, for mastery. They are challenge seekers.

I could name many examples which I have personally observed.
A client of mine in the South, for instance, is president of a
construction company. He is getting along in years and could
easily retire comfortably, leaving the company in the hands of
some very competent individuals. But if he retired he wouldn't

know what to do with his life. He tells me he will continue in the business "until they carry me out of here, because in this office, I'm the pro. I'm operating in my own ballpark. I know the rules here better than anyone else, and I want to run this game and manage this team." Nothing else could give him the same charge and satisfaction.

How your "action system" helps

This man, like most top executives, is driven by a need for mastery and competence. Beyond that, I like to think of his motivational drive as an "action system." What drives him is a *blending* together of the head, the heart, and the gut, and his understanding of the role and use of each.

There are some psychologists who believe that man is a creature of the physiological drive; some say he is a creature of the environment or a creature of his own mind. My position is that driven, successful businessmen are constantly blending external and internal forces, each of which has an influence on behavior. I regard the head, the heart, and the gut as a single "action system."

Here's another example of the drive for competence in another field: Recently, playwright Noel Coward reached his mid-sixties. Though he had suffered for years from gastritis, Coward stubbornly refused to slacken his pace. Noting his activities on the stage and television, the London *Times* wrote: "Here is a craftsman who has remained at the top of his profession . . . simply because he has dedicated his life not to attitudes or to transient theatrical movements but to getting on with his work to the best of his ability." Translation: Noel Coward is driven by a need for mastery.

Dealing with your drives

If all these things are true, the question then becomes, "How do you deal more effectively with your drives?"

Most obviously, it simply isn't enough just to *be* busy. It isn't enough to *have* high energy expenditure. A man who has a high level of activity is not necessarily dealing effectively with his en-

vironment. It is possible to be very self-confident, and to be extremely active, with little expenditure of energy. Voltaire, the
18th century French writer, philosopher, and businessman, had
very little physical energy. Physically he was a wreck. He had
contracted tuberculosis from his mother in infancy, suffered at
various times from smallpox, gout, rheumatism, deafness, blind-
ness, paralysis, and a host of other diseases and debilitations.
Yet, he was able to mobilize his unique talent. He made a fortune
by lending money, by speculating, by getting involved in shady
deals, by selling textiles and jewelry, and he acquired world re-
nown through his literary talent and debates. Most of Voltaire's
activities were conducted *not* by the expenditure of physical,
peripatetic energy. Rather, he was an unusually well organized
man.

Avoid being "busy"

I know many executives who are always busy. They are devoted to their companies; they work hard. You can count on them
to give their last ounce of effort to any project. *They're always
running.*

But their common problem is that even while expending so
much energy, they aren't getting the job done. They're always
putting out small fires, while the big ones rage uncontrolled.
These men are driving for competence and mastery. But chances
are they will never succeed. Being busy isn't enough. *You have
to direct your efforts; you have to channel your energies.* Otherwise, all the energy and output you generate will be dissipated.
You can't win the race unless you run on the track.

How do you run on the track? How do you channel your energies? How can you become more effective in dealing with
your environment, your business situations, and your subordinates? The balance of this chapter will bring you some practical
suggestions to help you answer these questions.

The advantage of the slight edge

I'll state the point immediately, even though you may question
its simplicity:

The slight edge makes the big difference. The successful and effective individual is often *only a little bit better* than his rival who fails to make the grade.

Dr. David Wechsler is chief psychologist in the psychiatric division of New York City's Bellevue Hospital. His book *The Range of Human Capacities* is the most authoritative work on this subject. The layman would find it difficult to read because it involves statistical studies of the differences in skill that characterize human beings. But his startling conclusions are readily understandable.

In strictly scientific terms, he reports that:

> The differences which separate the mass of mankind from one another, with respect to any one or all of their abilities, are small. . . . As compared with other ratios or orders of differences met within nature, they are pitifully insignificant.
>
> In a world where forces, velocities and distances exist, which are thousands, nay millions of times as great as those of any others with which they may be compared, one cannot, except by sheer arbitrariness, fail to accede that the differences met with in human beings are anything but insignificant. One need not turn to astronomy for contrasting examples; the realm of living things teems with illustrations. How small are the variations in human stature compared with those to be found in the heights of trees, the differences in the physical strength amongst men when compared with that of the elephant, or of his speed of locomotion when matched with the flight of birds . . .

But as Dr. Wechsler points out, it is certainly true that the small differences that exist within the range of human capacities produce big effects. The difference between 5 feet 11 inches and 6 feet 0 inches is admittedly small, but the ability to jump this extra inch may save a man's life.

In more humorous terms, Dr. Wechsler says that if Cleopatra's nose had been only a fraction of an inch longer, the face of Europe might have been changed because Caesar might have shown less interest in the lady. This is another example of how the size of the difference can be small, but the size of the consequences can be huge.

A cosmic example of the big difference that results from the slight edge is given in this account by Arthur C. Clarke, a British scientist, on why the U.S. failed in its first space probes while the Russians took the lead:

"To escape completely from the earth's gravitational field, a rocket must attain a speed which, in round figures, is 25,000 miles an hour. At a fraction less than this speed it must fall back to earth. At a fraction more, it has attained the freedom of space. The first Army and Air Force shots missed the crucial figure by only about 2 per cent, but that was enough. Then came the Russian moon probe, which beat it by about the same slim margin, and that was enough to take it not merely to the moon but, at the extreme end of its orbit, around the sun, more than 200,000,000 miles from earth, or almost 1,000 times as far away as the moon."

Actually, the philosophy of the slight edge, though it's rarely discussed in these words, is one of the most important aspects of corporate success. Differences in quality between various products are real, but usually in the same dimension as Cleopatra's nose. The differences are small, but they count.

Not "how much" but "how used"

For example, Swiss watchmakers don't rely on cheaper price to gain a big trading advantage over their competitors. Nor do they rely on lower labor costs. Instead, the Swiss turn out a *somewhat* better product so they can charge a much, much better price.

In baseball, the difference between a .300 hitter and a .250 hitter (one who makes $40,000 a year and one who makes $10,000 a year), is only a quarter-inch up or down on the bat.

What you have to recognize is that this little, apparently insignificant difference, in reality, makes all the difference in the world. Therefore, you must capitalize on *your* slight edge. Where *you* are slightly better than someone else, pounce on that difference and make it pay off. Exploit the opportunity. If you are slightly better than your peers at communicating with employees, then look for opportunities to do so more often; if you are slightly better at writing technical reports, try to write a few more than you have in the past; if you are a slightly better public speaker than your boss, ask if he won't permit you to take over some of his speaking chores for him; if your math is slightly better than that of all the other executives in your firm, remind the boss that you stand ready to help him review the financial reports.

Similarly, if the product you sell is only slightly better than that of your leading competitor, capitalize on the slight difference. Talk it up. Don't make a mountain of a molehill; don't exaggerate. But do emphasize that there *is* a difference.

Dr. Louis Rader, Group Vice-President of the electronics division of General Electric, reminded me of a stanza from a Kipling poem which underscores this point:

> And they asked me how I did it,
> So I gave them the scripture text;
> You keep your light so shining,
> A *little ahead* of the rest.

> And they copied all they could copy,
> But they couldn't copy my mind;
> And I left them striving and straining—
> A year and a half behind.

Isolate the important from the unimportant

Too often, in the pressures of business, managers are fraught with anxiety. Problems seem to crop up endlessly. It makes no difference how well the managers work, or in what order the problems are tackled—just *do* something!

But this is a self-defeating approach. Such a manager soon becomes fragmented in so many directions that his energy is dissipated. A more constructive approach would be to isolate the important from the unimportant, determining which projects have priority; then, channel all the effort and energy into the most important project of the moment.

Alcoholics Anonymous has a prayer that has brought many men back to sanity. It reads as follows:

O God, give me the serenity to accept the things I
cannot change.
Give me the courage to change the things I can and
ought to change, and,
O God, give me the wisdom to know the difference.

Knowing the difference can be difficult, particularly when
everything cries for your attention and your boss is breathing
down your neck. But you have to be able to function as if there
will be a tomorrow, and less important jobs can be put off until
then. Rationalize for this acceptable form of procrastination by
telling yourself, "Sure, I'm putting it off. But I know that by
putting it off, it will get better attention tomorrow when I can
devote more time to it."

I wouldn't be truthful with you if I did not acknowledge that
by so doing, you may create some problems. Yes, inevitably,
tomorrow will bring its deadlines and its pressures, and the
project you put off until tomorrow may not get the kind of
treatment you think it deserves. In fact, in my college classes,
I frequently tell my students, "When you're studying there's no
tomorrow, because tomorrow will hit you with other deadlines,
other pressures, other lessons and other tests—and every day
it gets worse, not better."

I cannot deny that conflict *is* created, but I can report a way
to resolve the conflict. A company president of my acquaintance
has set up a system for settling low-priority items that his executives put off until "tomorrow." He asks his executives to work
on Saturday mornings to clean up the little items that got shunted
aside during the week. (Yes, he pays his executives well!)

Each executive has two files on his desk. One is marked "Immediate" and one is marked "Saturday." Typically, the Saturday
file gets all the paperwork and questions that can wait until then
in the light of more urgent problems and paperwork. On Saturday, those files are cleaned out. They must be; for on Monday,
the routine starts all over again.

Sometimes, of course, the Saturday files get too fat. This means
only one thing; the executives aren't making the proper differentiation between what should be done immediately and what can

wait. They aren't setting priorities—they're *really* procrastinating.

Ten ways to maximize energy and drive

Here are ten suggestions for dealing effectively and confidently with your daily business affairs. Each one can add to the efficient use of energies and clear the way for increased impact.

1. RECOGNIZE THE IMPORTANCE OF SOME INEFFICIENCY

Stay flexible. Don't be so efficient that you can't flex and change with a shift in the wind. Don't become so stuck on one project or one method of operation that you couldn't move on to something else. I have found that executives who are very efficient on one kind of project or in one kind of activity, generally are useless in other situations. Rare is the executive who does *everything* well, who is perfectly suited to every job. A small degree of inefficiency helps a man to survive when the environment changes.

If you would take the time to trace the development of living things from earliest times, you would make a very interesting observation. You would find that the most efficient plants and animals were among the first to die out and become fossils. Some plants and animals were so efficient in one kind of environment, that when the environment changed they were unable to adapt themselves. They became extinct. The plants and animals that survived were those which were somewhat inefficient—adaptable. Reptiles, for example, are not very efficient on either land or in water. But alligators, lizards, snakes and frogs have survived through the eons simply because they are adaptable to either environment.

2. SET EFFECTIVE GOALS

Throughout this book you will find constant reference to the setting of effective goals. Goals and objectives are essential to the proper conduct of business and of the self, and I cover the subject in detail elsewhere, principally in Chapter Eight. However, relative to the economical use of energy, I want to make this point: Set a goal for yourself and your department that is slightly above that which you have previously attained, or slightly above that which you know positively you could attain with reasonable effort.

Ideally, a goal should keep you reaching. It recedes a little as you advance, allowing you enough success so that you have the confidence to go on. Thus, as you attain your goal, you should establish a new one just out of reach.

Alfred J. Marrow, a company president with a Ph.D. in psychology, once set up an interesting experiment in his factory. Marrow was interested, as are most businessmen, in having new employees reach optimum performance as quickly as possible. He began to try different methods of motivating his new and unskilled employees to reach standards of skilled performance.

With one group, Marrow set a goal that was difficult to achieve. He ordered the unskilled workers to reach their quota within 12 weeks after they were employed. Interestingly, after 14 weeks the group had reached only 66 per cent of standard performance. The individuals of this group missed their goals by about one-third.

With the second group that was equally unskilled, Marrow established *weekly* goals. The goals were progressive; that is, each was slightly more ambitious than the goal of the previous week. As the level of the employees' proficiency increased, the goals were advanced. At the end of 14 weeks, the average member of the second group had reached a standard of proficiency equal to that of a skilled operator!

Dr. Kurt Lewin, who founded the Research Center for Group Dynamics at MIT, believes that this experiment has much to teach executives and businessmen, particularly managers who supervise the production of others. "A successful individual," says Lewin, "typically sets his next goal somewhat, but not too much, above his last achievement. In this way he steadily raises his level of aspiration. Although in the long run he is guided by his ideal goal, which may be rather high, nevertheless his real goal for the next step is kept realistically close to his present position." Lewin says that the unsuccessful individual tends to make one of two mistakes: He may set his goal very low, often below his past achievement, or "he sets his goal too far above his ability. The latter conduct is rather common."

3. PREPARE YOURSELF

One of the best ways to mobilize your talent is to know the issues at stake and prepare more thoroughly than anyone else to deal with them. I know one executive, a company president, who goes to extremes to prepare himself every time his firm approaches a merger. This man trains himself, physically, just like a prize fighter: no drinking, no late hours, plenty of sleep, and good (but non-fattening) food. He starts weeks in advance of the negotiations. Why? He told me that he wants to maintain a keen mental edge. "I'm not going to let any slips go by," he said smugly, and of course the results are always good. He rarely makes mistakes in his merger negotiations.

When Arthur Goldberg was Secretary of Labor under John Kennedy, it was said that he never went within 100 feet of the President without having all his documents in order, fully prepared to answer any reasonable question Kennedy might ask.

4. DON'T TRY TO BE AN EXPERT IN EVERYTHING

You can't be, and it is foolish to try. Few men achieve greatness in many fields — da Vinci and Edison are among the rare ones who come to mind. But it is very difficult for most of us to do several things and do them all equally well. The man who becomes an expert in one field, and admits that he knows little or nothing about other fields, is far more respected than he who claims to know much about many subjects.

Best bet is to have different yardsticks for yourself when you participate in many activities. Apply a *tough* criterion to your specialty; relax the standards a little when you are not operating within your specialty.

For example, you may be a crack decision-maker, a top executive earning top money. When you get out on the golf course, does it make sense to kill yourself trying to play like Arnold Palmer? When you're on the dance floor, do you have to glide with the grace of Arthur Murray? Of course, you should try your

best, but *recognize that you don't have time to be a pro in everything.* Like Charlie Chaplin says, "We're all amateurs; we don't
live long enough to be professionals."

The advantage of leisure-time activities is that you can relax
the standards. You know that you don't have to be great to be
successful, and if you accept this concept, then almost any leisure
activity can be fun no matter how inadequate you are at it. I
haven't stopped playing golf, even though I rarely break a hun-
dred. I am satisfied with less-than-competence in order that I
may enjoy the exercise, relax, and return to my real work re-
freshed and better able to function.

5. KNOW YOUR ABILITIES AND ACCEPT YOUR LIMITATIONS

Admit that you're human, that you are subject to rage, the sex
drive, to self-defeating actions. Don't try to be a great storyteller
if you're an inadequate raconteur. Don't try the pressure sales
pitch if you're good at low-pressure sales. You have to allow
yourself a few weaknesses. Acceptance is not resignation. Heed
this advice from the philosopher Gracian:

"Recognize the piece that you lack. There are many who, if
they did not lack some attribute, could reach the peak of perfection... Some lack earnestness, a lack which can tarnish great
gifts. Others lack suavity of manner, a fault which soon lowers
the esteem felt for them, even though they are of high estate.
Some want executive ability; others want restraint. All these
disabilities, if they are recognized and heeded, could be com-
pensated for easily, and soon, with care, the compensation could
become the natural person."

6. APPRAISE YOUR EFFECT ON OTHERS

Everyone needs to get some feedback from others to know the
degree of his personal impact. Favorable feedback of course is
easier "to take" but sometimes unfavorable feedback can be more
valuable since it makes improvement possible.

For example, I get a lot of unfavorable feedback from my
friends. In fact, my best friends are the ones who tell me when
I've made mistakes. Sometimes it's painful or uncomfortable, but

I'm grateful for the feedback. Because if I *continued* to make mistakes, I'd really be in trouble.

You can't expose your anxiety by asking bluntly, "How am I doing?" In such cases, you are not likely to get thoughtful and objective answers. A better way to appraise how others regard you is to examine the kinds of problems people ask you to solve. Obviously, if they bring you tough problems, they think highly of you. On the other hand, if a man doesn't think highly of you at all, he will never ask for your advice and counsel.

Watch people when you talk to them. What are they doing? Paying attention? Looking for excuses to leave? Are they easily distracted? What kind of information do your friends, superiors and subordinates call to your attention? What memos do you receive? What activities do your friends ask you to join them in?

The object of all this is to develop an awareness of the world about you and how you fit in—your impact on your environment. The surprises in life are natural, but you don't want to catch more than your share. You don't want to get shocked, as Jefferson Davis did, when he suddenly discovered that other people did not consider him one of the world's greatest generals. Davis was functioning blindly.

7. REPEAT YOUR SUCCESSES

By the time you have reached the middle rungs of the executive ladder, you must have observed when your behavior wins you success and acceptance, and when it doesn't. Pick out those things that you like to do, that others like to see you doing, and that bring you success. Concentrate on them.

By the same token, isolate those areas in which you are less than likely to succeed, and don't waste your time and effort in those activities unless you are committed to them. Play on your strengths. A small, slightly built boy would be foolish to waste his energy at football, when he *knows* he could play baseball with greater chances of success.

8. LEARN TO LIVE WITH FAILURES

You'll never gain self-confidence just by telling yourself what you can do to achieve it. Try some of the lessons you've learned. If you fail, try again. Simply by chance alone, if you try often enough, you may win some of the time.

Many famous people found success by picking themselves up and starting all over again, even after miserable failures. They recognized that all of life is a learning experience, that in losing, they learned something that might prevent them from losing again. In trying to make a storage battery, Edison tried a thousand things that didn't work, but he persisted. He said, "Okay— now I know a thousand ways I *can't* make a battery."

The real measure of a pro is that he doesn't look at life in terms of success or failure, but in terms of a learning experience. The pro then practices what he learns.

Only by exposure, by making mistakes and risking loss, can a man learn things. When John Kennedy lost a bid for the Democratic vice-presidential nomination in 1956 to Estes Kefauver, he didn't quit. He said, "Okay, now we know the mistakes we made; we know what we have to do to win. In 1960 we'll go for the big job."

Of course, too much failure can result in a retreat. Perhaps you are practicing the wrong function, or perhaps you are trying to achieve too much in the right function. If the latter appears to be the case, then you are not setting your goals properly. Try taking smaller steps, doing the little things first. If you still fail, then acknowledge your limitations and stop trying to be a pro in that particular activity.

9. GET YOURSELF A GOOD MANAGER OR A HELPFUL COACH

Find someone who will help you appraise yourself honestly, who can help you see things objectively. Make sure he is the kind of man, for example, who can tell you whether you have failed too often to continue, or if you should persist with new knowledge.

A good manager or coach is also the kind of person who pushes you just enough but not too much, who needles you into trying a little harder without antagonizing you, who stands by to assist you when you need help. A good sales manager performs these functions. So does an understanding wife, a good company president, an industrial psychologist, or an old school chum or drinking buddy.

A friend of mine, for instance, had been with a company for 20 years. He was secure and confident, but he was given a big opportunity to go into business for himself. He had $25,000 of capital to invest. He was bright, capable, and had the required background. *I pushed him into the venture.* He would not have gone if someone had not added a little courage. (Naturally, I wouldn't have told you this if he had not turned out to be very successful.)

10. PAY ATTENTION TO DETAILS

In concluding this chapter on mobilizing executive drive, I want to remind you that neither success nor self-confidence will come easy. It is hard work.

When you see a professional baseball player make the tough ones look easy, you forget the years of practice, the hundreds of hours of drill, the torture of training, that went into the making of the tough play. Preparation, training, and practice are indispensable, *but no more so than paying attention to details.* My friend who trains physically for corporate mergers is a fanatic for details. That's why he rarely fails, and never makes the costly mental slips.

Ara Parseghian, the great Notre Dame football coach who successfully reversed the school's football fortune, is a fanatic for detail, training, preparation, and practice. I quote from an article in *Time*: "For Ara Parseghian, the man who cannot stand to lose, the day begins at 5:30 a.m. with four cups of coffee, usually ends with a tranquilizer and the late late show. Even when he eats, he has a pencil in the other hand, diagramming a play. Is there something he has forgotten, some minuscule detail he has overlooked, some new way to win?"

One of my clients is John Pardi, the president of Prosperity Cleaners, a large laundry and dry cleaning chain on Long Island. Pardi often walks into a store or through his plant on informal "inspections." When he sees something as minor as a blown light bulb or a puddle of water, he gets very excited. He reasons as follows: If the light bulb is out, then the employees are not concerned about their working conditions; if this is so, then they don't care about their jobs; if this is so, then they may be careless about their work or about their customers; if this is so, then the supervision is probably inadequate.

Pardi says, "I may be wrong, yes. But if I see every minor problem, every little detail, every headache as a symptom of cancer, then I am forced to check it out. I want to know whether it is malignant or benign."

An easy way of life? No, emphatically not. But for the business executive, with the drive to get to the top, there's nothing as rewarding. For many, in fact, no other way seems conceivable.

4.

Using Your Business Maturity
To Get More
Out of Your Job

Psychologists and psychiatrists are all agreed on this: The clue to personal success is the growth, or the progressive achievement, of emotional maturity.

While no one is likely to quarrel with that statement, few people are certain they know what a mature person looks like—his make-up, the way he meets the challenge of his job and his family responsibilities, his outlook on the world.

That stage of development which we generally refer to as maturity implies the ability to respond to a variety of stimuli without resorting either to a fight or a flight from problems. When a man is mature he is able to deal with problems objectively. His interests are broader and deeper than mere survival. He is able to operate with a degree of independence and a firm sense of reality.

Obviously, then, maturity is a tremendous asset. In fact, on or off the job, the word maturity has become a glittering seal of approval, a stamp of having what it takes. What is maturity—really?

IS IT A MATTER OF INTELLIGENCE?

No, maturity is not necessarily related to intelligence. A man may know the *Encyclopedia Britannica* by heart—and still be infantile in his emotions. All of us have known brilliant people who are like children in controlling their feelings, in their over-powering need for affection from everybody they meet, in the way they handle themselves and others, or in their response to frustration.

But brilliance of intellect is no handicap to mature emotional development. Evidence suggests quite the contrary: bright people tend to effect superior emotional and social adjustments.

IS A MATURE PERSON ALWAYS HAPPY?

No. Some people *think* that maturity means happiness. But Freud believed that unhappiness is not necessarily a sign of neurosis. Emotional maturity does not guarantee freedom from worry and difficulty. Emotional maturity is demonstrated by the way conflicts are solved, by the way pain is handled. People who are mature view their difficulties not as "disasters" but as "challenges."

IS THE GOAL THE SAME FOR EACH INDIVIDUAL?

A definition of maturity in Webster's Dictionary helps to clarify a point: "Mature—to advance towards perfection." The preposition is "towards," not "to." We can never arrive at perfection, but we can advance towards it.

Further, the changes and growth of an individual as he advances towards maturity must be uniquely his own. Guidelines, such as the following, can be provided. But each person must set up his own program. As the geneticist Dobzhansky points out, "Evolution is not striving to achieve some foreordained goal; it is not the upholding of predetermined episodes and situations—evolutionary changes are *unique*, *non-recurrent*, and *creative*."

IS IT A SPECIFIC POINT IN DEVELOPMENT?

A fourth common misconception is that maturity is a specific point in the curve of development. It is not. Actually, maturity is not a static state of being. It is more a state of becoming. This helps to explain why a man may handle one situation with maturity and become childishly emotional in another situation. Or as one executive put it, "I know I act with maturity in my job but I must admit that I'm an immature husband and an erratic father."

Recognizing signs of maturity in yourself and others

No executive is capable of reacting to all situations and all aspects of his life with complete maturity 100 per cent of the time. However, executives do handle many of their problems maturely. The qualities usually found in the mature, then, can be pinpointed. No single individual is likely to have all of them—but all are worth striving for.

1. HE ACCEPTS HIMSELF

The most effective executives are those who have a fairly good view of their strengths and weaknesses. In fact, this is essential to executive success; only the mature executive will surround himself with people to compensate for his own deficiencies. Since he can view himself objectively and realistically, he is able to make the most of his own endowments and is free from the frustration of trying to be what he is not.

Many executives spend hours around a conference table trying to impress each other rather than trying to find a solution for the problem at hand. Commenting on such a meeting, the president of one company says, "I don't waste my energy trying to impress others with my intellect or my background. I know that neither is my particular stock in trade. But I do get a kick out of impressing them with the size of my balance sheet, with which I can choke a horse."

Most people find it easier to admit their strengths than to concede their weaknesses. The mature man recognizes that he has deficiencies. People who know themselves with true, mature self-knowledge accept the positive and the negative. But on balance they believe in themselves because they know what they can be counted upon to accomplish. Essential to this acceptance is the recognition that the mature executive is constantly struggling to become better in order to fulfill his unique potential. He does not desire to emulate others, but to fulfill himself.

Dr. Abraham Maslow, who has spent many years of research on the elements of the healthy personality, points out, "The mature person wants to be the best he can be. In this area he has no competitors."

2. HE RESPECTS OTHERS

An executive must function within the framework of other people's strengths, weaknesses, abilities, and deficiencies. If he is mature, he respects these differences and doesn't try to mold others in his own image. He accepts the fact that each man adds his own qualities to the final mixture.

This does not mean the mature executive is soft-hearted. Accepting others does not mean coddling them forever if their shortcomings interfere with the overall goal. The executive who is mature can fire a man who does not contribute to the good of the organization. It is unfair both to the company and to the man who is failing not to terminate the association.

"Each should be free to find a better mate," is the way one executive expresses it. Or, as another puts it, "A man must appreciate under my guidance; if he depreciates, then it's unfair to keep the relationship going."

Perhaps the most frequent evidence of respect for others is the mature man's unwillingness to manipulate people. Office politics is a game he has no patience with. Raymond T. Hickok, president of Hickok Pioneer Manufacturing Co., says, "I will always be allergic to the subordinate who drives wedges between people. I believe that good executives should be building bridges."

3. HE ACCEPTS RESPONSIBILITY

The immature cry out against their fate. Their failures are caused by someone else; luck is against them; the odds are never on their side. The mature man recognizes and accepts the responsibilities and restrictions of situations in which he finds himself.

He recognizes, for example, that people need strength and someone to lean upon in times of difficulty, and that the responsibility for communicating that strength is his alone.

Responsibility, points out Joe Crail, president of Coast Federal Savings and Loan Association, is "the feeling that the individual is personally responsible for the success of all activities with which he is associated. It is the urge to do or get done what ought to be done. Believing in Santa Claus, luck, a minister, a superior, or anyone else to solve one's problem is a sign of immaturity. Believing in personal responsibility in one's own life is necessary for security and happiness."

4. HE IS CONFIDENT

Mature executives welcome the participation of others, even in the area of executive decision. Since they are confident of their own ability, they find it easy to recognize that others have ideas. Strength in others is a threat only to the insecure.

A mature executive gains deep satisfaction from the accomplishment of his juniors. He finds a sense of pride—together with the sobering awareness of responsibility, in realizing that his subordinates depend upon his leadership. Ambitious executives may well feel a twinge of pain in switching from the command to the counselor role or in stepping aside to make room for a subordinate to grow. However, the mature learn to find a sense of personal gain and satisfaction in contributing to the development of another man's potential.

The birth of just such mature understanding in one company president resulted from serious illness. His company was in the midst of many pressing problems when he suffered a heart attack. The production manager, who was a comparative newcomer, stepped in and took over most of the president's responsibilities. Since he was effective, ambitious, and aggressive, others in the organization were willing to let him take the lead.

However, upon the president's return, misgivings, jealousy, and resentment began to corrode the cooperation which previously had been willingly given. Plots, counter-plots, accusations, and rumors began to find their way to the president's ears. The easiest solution, recommended by many in the executive group, would have been to get rid of the disrupting influence of the production manager. There were strong hints that he was using his newly acquired power to the president's detriment.

Fortunately, the president acted with maturity. In an open meeting he confronted the entire group, called a halt to the politicking and backbiting. He formally spelled out the limits of authority and responsibility, and asked for the kind of loyalty they had all given so freely during his absence.

Had the president been anxious about his own loss of power, he might have let a good man go. Acting with maturity, he was able to retain all available energy and intelligence in the executive group and direct them toward effective functioning of the organization.

5. HE HAS PATIENCE

The mature executive learns to accept the fact that for some problems there are no easy solutions. He is not likely to embrace the first solution that suggests itself. He respects the facts and will try to assemble all available information before suggesting a cure. Not only is he willing to be patient, he recognizes that he is better off with more than one plan of action.

Robert S. McNamara, former president of Ford Motor Company and now Secretary of Defense, is a man who dislikes to act when only one course of action is open to him. He insists on options—three, four, or even more recommended possibilities to choose among; he is also patient in waiting out the receipt of the options from his subordinates. Those who know McNamara and his work unequivocally state that he is a superb administrator.

6. HE MAINTAINS HIS SENSE OF HUMOR

"To laugh is to be healthy." The mature person agrees with this maxim. But he doesn't joke at the expense of other people. Nor does he laugh when other people are hurt or when someone else is made to look silly or inferior.

Emotionally healthy people remember that humor should be good-natured, producing a warm smile and nice glow. Alben Barkley was famous for his ability to use this type of gentle yet penetrating humor, often at his own expense. He would tell how he had to spank his son one day for a minor offense. Using the ancient alibi of parents, he said to the boy, "You know, I'm doing this for your own good." And the lad responded, "Some day, Dad, I hope to return the favor."

Your sense of humor reveals your attitude toward people. The mature person uses humor not as a bludgeoning hammer but as a plane to smooth off the rough edges. In this respect Lincoln was the master craftsman. On one occasion, he was visited by a delegation that came to criticize. He sent them away mollified, saying, "Gentlemen, suppose all the property you were worth was in gold and you had put it in the hands of Blondin to carry across the Niagara River on a rope. Would you shake the cable or keep shouting at him, 'Blondin, stand up a little straighter; Blondin, stoop a little more?' No, you would hold your breath, as well as your tongue, and keep your hands off until he was safely over."

Of course, the acid test of sense of humor lies in the ability to laugh heartily at one's own expense. Charles Yelin, a vice-president of Hickok Pioneer, was in an airplane crash on a flight from Rochester to New York City. Miraculously, he survived. He was lying in the grass, dazed and bleeding, when a reporter ran over and asked him, "Do you have a statement for the press?" Yelin looked around at the smoking ruins of the Mohawk Airlines plane, looked down at his own state of disarray, and suddenly the reporter's question tickled his sense of the ridiculous. "Yes," he said, "Fly American!"

7. HE HAS RESILIENCY

All of living has its share of illness, pain, disappointment. Not even the mature can escape this burden. However, the mature man bounces back from life's hurts with hope and with resiliency. He does not pretend that all is well, but he accepts the fact that pain must be borne, mistakes corrected, and he wastes no time agonizing over the past.

Failures and defeats that might crush a lesser man are viewed as lessons from which the mature man learns. For example, a large metropolitan bank had invested considerable time and money investigating the desirability of installing data processing equipment. After the initial survey and selection of equipment, two men were given complete responsibility for supervising the change-over. They were instructed to take as much time as they felt they needed and to move only when they felt all problems had been eliminated.

Eager to make a good impression, they underestimated the morale factor. The result: chaos. Finally the president asked the men for a full report. One executive offered essentially a defense of his own behavior. He pinned the blame for problems on every available donkey.

The second man started from the premise that he had been seriously mistaken in his original estimate of the personnel factors involved. Then he proceeded to outline a well-thought-out plan for carrying out the change-over from this point on, repairing the damage done, and avoiding the traps of their first efforts. For him the fiasco had been transformed into a learning and growing experience.

8. HE CAN MAKE DECISIONS

Side by side with his patience in searching out solutions, the mature executive is able, when necessary, to make a decision in spite of ambiguity. Having weighed the facts, he recognizes that there is a time when action must be taken; a time, in fact, when indecision amounts to a decision not to act. Then, relying on his confidence in himself and the people around him, he is willing to take a calculated risk.

Management authority Peter Drucker points out that with regard to the future there can never be certainty, only possibilities. The mature executive who must plan for the future learns to accept this. He makes decisions on the basis of the best available estimates, for he knows that if he waits for complete certainty he may miss the boat altogether.

9. HE IS INTEGRATED

The mature man is not a person fragmenting his energies by moving in ten different directions simultaneously. But because he is an organized person, he handles multiple problems effectively.

He is not thrown by the sudden need to shift gears, to move from one activity to another without confusion. Robert Bemer, an executive formerly of the Univac Division of Sperry Rand Corp., put it to me this way, "A machine tackles problems by moving sequentially from one stage to another without any interruption.

An executive cannot afford to perform in this fashion. For example, my secretary came in the other day while I was puzzling over a million dollar order. If I brushed her off and insisted on following my sequence, she'd throw sand in the works somewhere. I had to give her a modicum of attention by looping over and then coming back."

10. HE WELCOMES WORK

An emotionally healthy person knows how to enjoy his job. His is rarely a lazy life. He knows the satisfaction of doing things well and he takes pride in his accomplishments.

Here again, there is little difference among mature people, no matter what their walk in life. Appreciation of one's work is characteristic of the mature scholar and the mature bricklayer, the artist and the cook, the engineer and the lathe operator, the statistician and the stenographer. Each gets satisfaction out of life once he stops fighting his work and decides to enjoy it.

Just so, psychiatrist Abraham Meyerson points out that even the simplest discovery comes from diligence. "A scholar," says Meyerson, "is like a pin, which as you know, must have a good sharp end as well as a good round end. The scholar's sharp end is to think with, his round end is to sit down to the job with. If he has only the sharp end, he becomes a dilletante flitting from job to job, accomplishing little. If he has only the round end, he is a pendant, unimaginative and uninspired."

In an executive group it is rare to find a man who fears work. The danger lies in the other direction. Many executives use their work as an escape, a hiding place from other problems, a compensation for disappointment in their personal lives. Such compulsive drivers may be valuable to their companies, but they do injustice to themselves.

Work, for some executives, is a place to hide; for others it may be a way of guaranteeing their future monument. Work, for a *mature* executive, is often like the dedication of a mature scientist. It is almost necessary for his survival as an individual. It is a way in which he communicates his self-image, and in which he guarantees his future. Through his work, he keeps himself from wallowing in his own anxieties.

11. HE HAS STRONG PRINCIPLES

One of the unifying forces in the mature personality is a strong sense of values and an underlying philosophy which serves as a guide for behavior. This ability to commit oneself to an idea, a cause, or a principle is a product of some of the other qualities of maturity: self-acceptance, the ability to weigh facts, the capacity to learn from experience.

For many businessmen, the company becomes the primary commitment. Many executives actually see the organization as a living thing with a life of its own beyond theirs. They view themselves as the guardians of the company's well-being. Their role is to nurture and protect it and pass it on to its future guardians.

This explains the apparent singleness of purpose with which many mature executives can make and carry out decisions. This accounts both for their involvement in the development of others and their ability to be tough when necessary.

One executive, commenting on this seeming paradox, points out that you can be tough or soft, as the situation dictates, when you are not doing it for any personal gain but for the future security of your company. As Dean Emanuel Saxe of the Baruch School of City College of New York put it, "The more a man believes in a principle, the more he will fight."

A man who is deeply committed is not likely to give up easily. The mature executive makes decisions which will help the organization to become more secure. He makes dynamic choices where the company's survival is concerned.

12. HE HAS A SENSE OF PROPORTION

The mature man lives a balanced life because he has a sense of perspective. He takes pride in his company and his position in it, but he also recognizes his role in the larger scheme of things. If he is able to work hard, he is also able to cut himself off from business pressures and enjoy his leisure.

A subordinate telephoned Marshall Rinker, Sr., president of Rinker Materials Corp., while he was on the golf course vacationing. Rinker returned the call from the club house at the end of the ninth hole.

He listened carefully as the subordinate explained the sticky situation. Then Rinker asked one question: "Are the others worrying?"

"They certainly are," was the answer.

"Well," he responded, relaxed again, "that's fine. If they're worrying then I can go back to my golf. I'll be in the office next week, and then I'll worry while they play."

That was maturity talking.

How to measure your maturity

Maturity is a process of becoming. To get some idea of your own maturity, you must look for signs of *growth*. Read the questions below and put a check beside the ones you can honestly answer "Yes." Remember, there are no scores, no right and wrong answers. However, if this check-list can help you see yourself objectively, you are on the way to that important first step: self-acceptance.

In the past year:

● Did you willingly accept responsibility for the mistakes of your subordinates?

● Did you cheerfully share credit with colleagues who helped you?

● Did you patiently listen to people you disagreed with?

● Did you re-examine at least one of the assumptions that you have always taken for granted?

● Did you manage at least one two-week vacation away from business?

● Were you able to accept unfavorable feedback about yourself?

● Were you less irritated with co-workers; did you find them easier to deal with?

● Did you take an unpopular stand on an issue you believed in?

● Did you experiment with at least one new idea?

● Did you welcome suggestions and discussion from subordinates?

● Did you feel confident that you could handle your problems?

● Did you feel at ease in meetings and conferences?

● Did you voluntarily accept a new challenge or an added responsibility?

● Did you attempt to improve your skills through reading, seminars, study?

● Did you develop an assistant capable of taking over for you?

● Did you explore new interests: social groups, hobbies, sports, etc.?

● Did you tend to help people more, criticize them less?

● Did you improve your ability to plan your time?

● Did you learn to delegate more of your work?

● Did you get along better with subordinates; feel less threatened by them?

● Did you lose your temper less frequently?

● Did you develop the ability to see humor in more situations?

● Did you find more time for your family?

● Did you come to any new conclusions about yourself?

● Did you acquire new friends?

● Did you change some of your opinions and feelings about things?

● Did you find it easier to live with problems for which you had no immediate solutions?

● Did more people seek you out for advice and assistance?

● Did you find that you accomplished more with less effort?

● Did you gain a stronger conviction about the basic truths, religion, or philosophy in which you believe?

5.

How to Understand
And Deal with
Defensive People

When the New York *Mirror* made the abrupt announcement that it was discontinuing publication, some 1,600 employees were suddenly face-to-face with a personal crisis.

According to reports from eyewitnesses, some staff members stoically continued to put the last issue of the paper "to bed." Some, with equal calm, closed their desks, gathered personal possessions and left the office immediately.

Some raced to phone booths to announce the shattering news to their wives. Others grabbed phones to contact friends and see if they could be first on line in the rush for new openings.

As a psychologist, I would bet that each acted according to a well-established pattern of personal behavior; acted, moreover, in a way that could have been predicted by a trained observer. For, each one of us is equipped with a kit of "defense mechanisms," an almost automatic way of responding to anything that presents a threat to the self.

Psychiatrists point out that if each of us were exposed to the full impact of all the stresses and strains of daily living, we would crack under the crushing pressures. Instead, the human mechanism has developed ways of screening out those things we cannot comfortably tolerate at the moment. What's more, it provides a "mask" behind which we can hide until we have the chance to regain control.

The man in the pressroom who stuck it out until the final pages had rolled off the press may very well have been operating under the mechanism known to psychologists as "denial;" pretending for the moment that nothing was changed. For him, standing by the rolling press provided reassurance that the world had not crumbled.

The reporter who rushed immediately to phone his wife was seeking the reassurance that loss of job would not mean loss of love. Thus, for him, threat set in motion the defense mechanism of flight into childhood, or regression.

Others responded to the news with anger and aggression. It was only natural that many would bitterly flail out against the company, trying to pin down blame. But such outbursts, too, served the useful purpose (for them) of letting off steam and emotional tension, thereby postponing full confrontation of the immediate problem until they were able to cope with it.

Every experienced executive has observed variations of all these defense behaviors at one time or other. The trigger need not be anything so extreme as loss of job. Pressures and tensions of far lesser degree will also bring these defense mechanisms into operation. The important thing for the executive to recognize is that these reactions are healthy; in fact, they may be nature's best method for *insuring* mental and emotional health.

For the executive whose effectiveness is inextricably bound up in his ability to work with others, knowledge of defense behavior is essential. This chapter aims to provide you with the information needed to help you become a more effective manager. And it's an interesting fact: once you digest the information in the pages ahead, you'll know more about other people as well as yourself.

Once you understand some of the human webs that entangle every manager, you'll be better able to control your emotions.

Somehow, even though there may be nothing you can do, it soothes the emotions, the wear and tear, if there's some insight about why people act the way they do. It's that feeling of flying blind that often causes emotional explosions.

Why we need our disguises

At some time or other, every individual feels the need to hide his inner feelings behind some sort of curtain or disguise. In fact, some psychologists claim that personality itself is a disguise. The very word, in fact, comes from the Latin "persona," which means facial disguises.

Long ago, actors wore masks to indicate the characters they played. The masks hid their real identities and showed the audience only what the actors wanted them to see. Like the players of old, we are all actors with our own special masks camouflaging our true selves.

The most obvious reason is that your behavior is guided by the need to be liked. You act in such a way as to look good in the eyes of your fellows. If strong men are popular, you strive to become strong. If being quick on the trigger is considered the top accomplishment, you will stay up nights developing this ability. No one is immune to the need to rate well in the eyes of other people: the boss, colleagues, families—but, most particularly, those whose opinions matter to you.

Psychologists have discovered that there is another opinion that is of utmost importance to each of us: *our own.* Consciously or unconsciously, we fight to protect our own good picture of ourselves. And in this fight, we may use a weird assortment of weapons: forgetfulness, alibis, excuses—even distortion.

To take a familiar example, consider for a moment the typical situation of a sales supervisor trying to read the riot act to his sales force after a particularly disappointing quarter. The more he hammers away on their inefficiency in planning, their lapses in product knowledge, their laxity in servicing accounts or any other selling weaknesses, the more he is bound to stir up resentment. The longer he dwells on their shortcomings, the more his attempt at motivation will boomerang.

For it is normal and natural for each man to fight against the idea that he can be guilty of so much wrong. The sales manager may mistake the reaction for resistance against him, but actually it will be a defense of the self-image that he has stirred up.

Always criticize the act and not the person

It is for this very reason that experts on counseling will advise that the counselor criticize the act and not the person. Not only is it more constructive to criticize in terms of behavior, which can be improved, but it is less likely to bring defensiveness into play.

Just by way of one more illustration of this point, let me turn back for a moment to the case of the *Mirror*. As soon as the union heard the announcement, it issued a heated statement that the company had violated its bargaining agreement by failing to discuss its plans in advance of closing down. Undoubtedly, the union officials were reacting to the implication that a recently settled strike had been a salient factor in the newspaper's demise.

Here again, what on the surface appeared to be an attack against the company was more accurately a fight on the part of the union officials to defend their reputations. To admit to past mistakes would be too damaging *in their own eyes.*

So too, will people sometimes project their own faults onto others, rather than admit *to themselves* that *they* might be guilty of the flaw. The man who is afraid to take risks may be the first to accuse others of having no guts. But if you understand the reason for his accusation of others, you will be in a better position both to evaluate his remarks and to help him cope with his own problem.

The secretary who criticizes other stenographers for "making a play for the boss" probably has an eye on him herself. But an understanding supervisor will recognize that her comments indicate a gnawing doubt about her own attractiveness. Rather than meet her gossipy remarks head-on, he will treat them as a symptom of a different problem and accordingly try to bolster her shaky self-confidence by treating her with a show of respect and consideration.

Why alibi artists act that way

Similarly, the alibi artist who has a ready reason why things went wrong, the chronic boaster who belittles every accomplishment other than his own, the buck-passer who manages to avoid responsibility—each in his own way is doing the same thing. He is not trying to kid you, he is not trying to make trouble for someone else, *he is fighting, the best way he knows how, to shield himself.* That others may incur blame or that others may be misled if he is successful, is only incidental to his purposes. He is, in a sense, engaged in a fight for survival—the survival of his own good opinion of himself. As Dr. Gardner Murphy, the famous psychologist at the Menninger Clinic, points out, "Human resources for protection against self-reproach are rich and varied."

I have described the defense mechanisms of human behavior as if they were separate and discrete entities. To understand defenses it is helpful to consider them separately; in practice, however, they overlap. Nothing will be as simple in practice as I have made it sound here.

How to see through others' disguises

The problem for the manager in dealing with defensive behavior is that he must understand the underlying reasons while at the same time avoid challenging or uncovering them.

Remember that people not only believe fully in their own best intentions, but such belief is vital to them. Gordon Allport, a Harvard psychologist, found that it is only the "rare person" who has insight into himself. Probably no more than one in 20 has the lucky faculty of seeing through his own mask. That's why it is easier sometimes for the trained observer to know more about people than they do themselves. Thus, the sensitive executive may understand a subordinate's motives more clearly than the junior man, himself. But it would be a fatal error for the superior to use this insight in a direct confrontation, even for the purpose of helping him improve.

For example, an executive in a key spot in a marine engine assembly plant talked for years about retiring. According to the old fellow, the company just couldn't find a suitable replacement. The fact of the matter was, however, that every time someone was suggested as a candidate, the retirement-bound executive found some fault with him. One was "too young to handle the men," another "didn't understand machinery," another lacked sufficient experience. Actually, it was clear to the other executives that the old man was afraid to let go of the reins. He had never prepared himself for a life of leisure, and he was really fighting against the idea of an empty future. But, after having talked of retirement for years, he couldn't admit to himself that he had any mental reservations either. His behavior was a desperate fight against facing up to the facts.

To force the issue by bluntly exposing the reasons for his behavior would be most destructive. However, an understanding boss, having insight into the problem, might bolster the man's self-respect and gradually ease him into an acceptance of retirement. One solution might be to provide him with some plans for the future; another might be to utilize his experience in a training position, where he would have the opportunity to prepare a group of younger men for increased responsibility. Allowing him to stay on in a supervisory or counselling role while his replacement took over would be constructive not only from the man's point of view, but from the company's as well.

Why defense mechanisms aren't weaknesses

I frequently find that executives tend to equate the concept of defense mechanisms with weakness. True, the man who resorts to a repeated pattern of alibiing or risk-avoidance may be acting out of weakness. However, it is just as often true that donning a disguise is a true act of courage and becomes a valuable source of strength.

Take, for example, the man who has deep feelings of inferiority because of physical weakness; he compensates by driving himself to excel. Theodore Roosevelt's reputation as a Rough Rider had its roots in the taunts and teasings of other children because he was a physical weakling as a child.

Other men might compensate for physical shortcomings by driving themselves intellectually. Many students conquer their doubts by driving and cramming and becoming successful "overachievers."

I have seen men find in a sales career the constant recognitions, victories, and approvals that their egos required. Every executive can point to examples of successful careers that owe a debt to the struggle for approval.

Just as frequently, the defensive disguise serves the important function of enabling a person to carry on in the face of great obstacles. The man who refuses to admit defeat may, by dint of stubborn effort, work his way through an impasse and accomplish the seemingly impossible.

The boundary line between what is desirable and what is undesirable—what is asset and what is liability—in the operation of defense mechanisms is not always clear-cut. Generally, however, it is a matter of degree.

The same defense mechanism that enabled thousands of people to sink to a level of passivity that carried them through the tortures of concentration camps and enabled them to emerge intact and reestablish their lives, also caused many to sink beyond caring forever.

In healthy doses, we blot out a painful episode by forgetting; thus, we are better able to carry on. In unhealthy degrees, the forgetting is carried to such extremes that a deeper withdrawal results. If the withdrawal amounts to a complete loss of contact with reality, then we have true mental illness.

But the executive will rarely be faced with such extreme cases on the job. More likely, he may have to contend with the sort of disguise that people use when they are temporarily reluctant to face facts. If the mask is sometimes used to "save face," remember that it also serves to put a more tolerable face on the world. An employee's resort to a defense mechanism is not, then, necessarily a matter of weakness. It may be wise of him to concentrate all his energies on the problems that he knows he can handle, and to provide himself with temporary relief from the others.

How an executive can deal with disguises effectively

Every executive can learn to recognize the symptoms of defense behavior in his colleagues and subordinates. More important than increasing your sensitivity, however, is learning how to control your own reactions. Here are some specific guides to keep in mind:

1. RECOGNIZE THAT DEFENSIVE BEHAVIOR IS NORMAL

Everyone will make excuses or repress an unpleasant memory on occasion. Accept such behavior as normal. An employee should not be banished from the circle of your good will merely because he hides behind these defenses from time to time.

2. NEVER ATTACK A MAN'S DEFENSES

The most damaging thing a supervisor can say to a subordinate is, "You know the real reason you're using that excuse is because you can't bear to be blamed for anything." Such attempts to "explain a man to himself" are bound to inflame more than they enlighten. Psychiatrists, who know the danger of sudden revelation, often take years breaking the news to a patient or opening his eyes to the reasons for his behavior.

3. DISCUSS FACTS, NOT PSYCHOLOGY

If you can, indeed, see behind a man's mask and truly understand the reason for his behavior, you can be most helpful by using this insight to help him satisfy his need in more valid ways. A man who compensates for his insecurity by boasting will benefit from your praise when you really think he's performing well. He'll have less need to brag then. Similarly, you can often help a man feel good about himself by pointing out specific ways in which he can improve his performance.

4. POSTPONE ACTION

Sometimes the best thing to do is nothing at all. People frequently react to sudden threats by instinctively hiding behind their masks. But, given sufficient time, a more rational reaction takes over. Another reason to wait out the first stage is that some defense mechanisms are mainly attention-getters. If the undesirable behavior fails to get the desired attention, the person may be discouraged from resorting to this behavior.

5. RECOGNIZE YOUR OWN LIMITATIONS

Don't expect to be able to solve every problem that comes up —especially the human ones. And remember that you, too, are human, and therefore all of these same mechanisms operate in your own life. Under certain pressures, you will also respond with anger and aggression; sometimes *you* will compensate. If you can use your insights to understand your own reactions better, you will be going a long way toward improving on-the-job relationships.

Most important, remember that no executive should ever try to be a psychologist. You have enough to do without undertaking emotional first aid. If you offer your people understanding, you are offering them a valuable climate for their own healthy growth.

6.

Managing Your
Executive Tensions

Preoccupation with the problem of tension is one of the characteristic phenomena of our society.

Executives, especially, are bombarded with advice from all sides concerning the inherent dangers of tension and stress. They are warned that business pressures make them more susceptible to all the physical diseases of mankind—high blood pressure, ulcers, cardio-vascular diseases, and coronary attacks. So general is this belief that bitter jokes refer to one-, two-, and three-ulcer jobs.

But if executives have a matter-of-fact acceptance of tension as an unavoidable part of their lives, so does everyone else! Tension is a popular topic everywhere, from commuter trains to cocktail parties: "I can't relax; I'm too tense." "I'd be lost without my tranquilizers." "That job will kill him; he's so wound up he's always on the verge of blowing his top."

Everyone is either watching his own individual worry barometer or, as one executive put it, "taking his colleagues' emotional temperatures." Dr. Norman Vincent Peale once observed, "The

American people are so tense that it is impossible to put them to sleep—even with a sermon!"

Measuring your own tension level

Do you consider yourself easygoing, or tense?

Tension-level can usually be measured by your reaction to everyday situations. Here are some statements from Dr. Janet Taylor's Manifest Anxiety Scale. Try to answer them as objectively as possible.

- I have often felt that I faced so many difficulties I could not overcome them.
- I am easily embarrassed.
- My feelings are hurt more easily than most people.
- I wish I could be as happy as others.
- I certainly feel useless at times.
- I feel anxious about something or someone almost all of the time.
- It makes me nervous to have to wait.
- At times I am so restless that I cannot sit in a chair for very long.
- Sometimes I become so excited that I find it hard to get to sleep.
- At times I have been worried beyond reason about something that really did not matter.
- I find it hard to keep my mind on a task or job.
- I am more self-conscious than most people.
- I am the kind of person who takes things hard.
- I am a very nervous person.
- Life is often a strain to me.

Answering too many questions in the affirmative is an indicator of high tension level.

Another list of questions, devised specifically for executives by Dr. William C. Menninger of the Menninger Foundation, may be even more useful in determining your tension threshold. Try some of these. They may take more time and thought, but they are worth considering as a measure of your on-the-job tension.

WHAT ARE YOUR PERSONAL RELATIONSHIPS LIKE?

Person-to-person contacts in the course of a day can ease or exaggerate other tension-building factors. In determining your own reaction to personal relations, consider:

- How well do you get along with your assistants?
- Are you known as a prima donna?
- All of us have had bad days, but how frequently do yours occur?
- Do your resentments smolder, resulting in frequent emotional outbursts?

HOW DO YOU DEAL WITH REALITY?

Smack up against the stone wall of facts, people react differently. Your tension threshold will be determined partially by your answers to these questions:

- Do you lose your temper and become panicky?
- Do the jitters prevent you from functioning?
- Or, in spite of inner tension, are you able to complete your day's work?

DO YOU ACCEPT FRUSTRATION?

"Smooth sailing" is a lovely phrase and a beautiful dream that we seldom encounter in our daily lives. The way we adjust to the frustrations of a less-than-perfect situation is important.

- How do you accept situations that block your goals?
- Are you able to wait for what you want, or are you the kind of person who, when he wants something, wants it now?
- If the going gets too tough, do you pick up your marbles and leave the game?
- Have you learned that one has to work and wait for most of the worthwhile things?

CAN YOU ACCEPT HELP?

While all give lip service to the idea that the rugged individualist is a thing of the past, the tense executive finds it difficult to accept this fact. Dr. Menninger asks, "Do you have the good judgment to seek expert assistance when tension gets beyond personal control?"

In my own experience, this vacillation between independence

and dependence is a key factor in the tension level of many sons of very successful fathers. One executive never got over the way his father made quick and correct decisions. After he inherited the business at a very early age without training, he emulated his father's pattern of rapid decision-making. Catastrophe resulted and the company lost millions of dollars.

Now the young man, much older (and wiser to the extent of an ulcer), is learning to modify his impulsiveness, and the company is making progress. However, to this day, he has trouble asking his executives for advice in critical times. He feels compelled to be the strong father figure—at the sacrifice of his health. He really wants the suggestions of others, but cannot bring himself to ask, for fear he might be less of a man compared to his father. He never achieved the ease of Tom Watson, Jr., who, having once been introduced as a "chip off the old block," immediately responded with "The block hasn't yet been chipped!"

Tension can make you sick

Physical stress can often be a kind of body language to express certain emotional conflicts. All of us know the phrases, "I got my back up," or "You give me a pain in the neck," or "That assistant of mine burns me up." These expressions are close descriptions of actual, physical reactions to emotion.

Some understanding of the physiology of stress may be helpful. The theory of what occurs within us during periods of stress is labeled the Cannon-Bard Theory of Emotions. Briefly stated, it is this: Whenever you are in a situation of threat, your body prepares to flee or to fight. In moments of peril everything gets into the act. First, messages from your eyes or ears get carried to the pituitary gland located at the base of the brain. It secretes a substance known as ACTH into the blood stream. ACTH triggers the adrenal glands, located above the kidneys, which further secrete substances known as cortisone. Then, everything within the body pops. First the heart beats rapidly. Muscles of the stomach and intestines contract, forcing the blood to circulate faster. Breathing speeds up. You are ready for the enemy!

A problem can be created when your body reacts in this fashion to a minor provocation. Your body prepares for a battle, when in actuality there is no real threat. This is physically harmful.

As Dr. Hans Selye, one of the foremost authorities on tension, points out, "Inadequate counter-measures in the face of serious attacks may be the cause of disease or death, but excessive defense reactions may likewise be harmful if they are quite out of proportion to the negligible threat."

Stress and the stomach

One of the most dramatic cases in medical history revolves around the study of Tom, a man whose gastric activities during periods of emotional stress were observed by Drs. S. G. and H. G. Wolfe over a period of seven months. Tom, a 57-year-old man employed in the Wolfe medical laboratory, had an opening made surgically into his stomach following an accident. The doctors were thus able to observe changes occuring in Tom's stomach.

One morning, an irate doctor asked Tom about some important papers he could not find. Tom had mislaid them. His face became pale. In his stomach, the rate of acid production necessary for food digestion dropped. However, this was not severe. Then Tom began to look for the papers—and found them. Satisfied, the doctor left the room. Tom's stomach wall immediately regained its former color; its normal flow of gastric juices resumed. No permanent damage occurred.

On another occasion, one of the doctors criticized Tom's work and suggested that he might be discharged. Outwardly, Tom accepted the rebuff politely. But internally he erupted like a volcano. His stomach became red and engorged, and soon the folds were thick and turgid. Acid production accelerated sharply and vigorous contractions began. Damage to Tom's body was significant, since there was no outlet for this stress.

Evidence such as this demonstrates the physical toll you pay for your tensions. Notice, however, that the quicker you are able to mobilize yourself and handle the threats or problems you face, the less physical damage you suffer. Ulcers and heart conditions need not be the price of success. Learning to fight the necessary battles—and only the necessary ones—can help you avoid the physical toll.

Tension and heart disease

Some experiments by Dr. C. Snyder, a Philadelphia scientist, indicate a linkage between tension caused by crowded living conditions and heart disease.

Dr. Snyder trapped 24 wild woodchucks and put them in small cages. Some had cages of their own; others were caged by pairs. Among the 10 having cages to themselves, only one died of heart disease. But of the 14 placed two to a cage, five died of heart disease. The stress of overcrowding was apparently the cause, according to Dr. Snyder. Similar experiments with chickens showed the same result.

Dr. Herbert Ratcliffe similarly suggests that grouping animals in large numbers leads to competition and stress, or "social interaction," as he terms it. Adrenal glands show changes characteristic of heightened stress. (The adrenals secrete chemical substances which help the body combat stress.)

Urban man may be encountering similar coronary-producing stresses in his struggles to "get ahead" and to cope with crowded living conditions. "The greater susceptibility of the human male in urban societies (to heart disease) possibly reflects his much greater mean exposure to economic competition," says Dr. Ratcliffe. However, in the animal experiments, individual reaction to stress varied considerably.

Former President Eisenhower explained his 1955 heart attack on the golf course in terms of tension. He told an interviewer that he received notice of a telephone call on the fourth hole, and drove back to the clubhouse in his cart. Then he learned that the State Department had been trying to reach him but would not be ready to talk for about an hour.

So he returned to his game. A few holes later he received notice of another urgent call. He discovered, when he got back to the clubhouse a second time, that it was still the first call. He returned again to his game.

Some time later he returned to the clubhouse and completed the call. Then he started on the second nine, only to be interrupted by still another call. This was from someone who did not know that he had already completed the business involved.

"I always had an uncertain temper, and by this time," he said, "it had gotten completely out of control. One doctor said that he'd never seen me in such a state—and that's the reason I had the heart attack. So I've never gotten angry again." Lucky is the man who can say that and mean it.

A fascinating study on this subject was conducted by Dr. Henry Murray of Harvard. He put subjects in situations where they agreed to criticize or be criticized while they took average heart rate measures. He found that, contrary to usual opinion, the heart rate is higher when a man is doing the criticizing than when he is under attack. It is the highest of all when subjects are "most talkative and most offensively aggressive." When a subject becomes the attacker himself, heart rate invariably jumps. Incidentally, in Dr. Murray's experiments the subjects seemed unaware of such changes.

Thus, destructive changes can take place without awareness. One executive, hearing about Murray's research, was overwhelmed by the implications. "If I respond to criticism and attack, I'll get a heart problem. But if I submit I may get an ulcer."

Fortunately, the choices are not limited to these two extremes, although many executives think so.

Wear and tear of stress

Dr. Hans Selye subdivides the effects of stress and its influence on the body into three stages. The first stage is your reaction to alarm. Responses are faster because the body is ready to help you respond. As the stress continues, you start to adjust to the pressure and recover your normal equilibrium. However, if the stress continues indefinitely, then the body completely collapses and exhaustion occurs.

This also provides insight into how our actions are affected by tension. In its early stages, the tension is beneficial since it mobilizes the physical and mental resources we need to overcome danger or grasp opportunity. But, if the tension is prolonged, our behavior deteriorates.

This graph, developed by Dr. John R. P. French, Jr., of the University of Michigan's Research Center for Group Dynamics, compares performance under stress to average performance. In the initial alarm stage, performance drops; it climbs as the individual enters the resistance stage. If the second stage is prolonged, however, performance once again suffers as the person moves into the final, or exhaustion, stage:

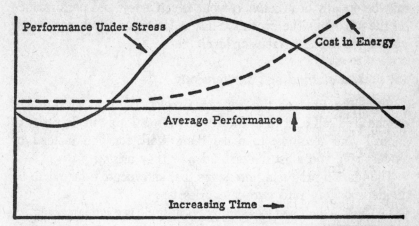

The effect of exposure to prolonged stress on a normal person's behavior has also been examined by Dr. Richard Lazarus and Dr. James Dees of Johns Hopkins University. In experiments with a group of students, each was asked to try to get out of a room with four doors. The subjects knew that one door would be unlocked on each trial, but they weren't told that the door which was unlocked one time, would never be unlocked the next. Over a series of trials, an alert subject could be expected to uncover and use that principle.

After a series of trials under ordinary conditions, the experimenters added various stresses—electrical shocks, cold showers, continuing blasts from a loud horn. The actions that resulted were classified into four types:

- A rational plan, such as "Do not push any door twice, do not push any door that was correct last time."
- A stereotyped plan, such as, "Go down the row, one, two, three, four, trying all doors."
- A repetitive plan, "Push one door repeatedly even though it fails to open."
- Irregular trial and error, "Push doors unsystematically."

As the tension was prolonged, stereotyped and repetitive plans increased. The subjects, although bright, all acted stupidly. The quality of their actions deteriorated. If the experiment had continued, the students would have succumbed to exhaustion.

So, tension is not only an enemy of health and well-being; it may be equally destructive of your effectiveness and performance on the job. Thus the executive has at least two good reasons for wanting to reduce his tension level.

Understanding your tensions

From the time of the ancient Greeks, Western culture has emphasized self-control as the key to personal growth. In order to control your tensions, to make them work for you instead of against you, you must understand why they arise.

The tension-producing pressures that an executive faces can be divided roughly into two categories:

1. Those which he faces simply because he is a human being.
2. Those which are a product of the executive's environment.

Dr. A. H. Leighton, in the *Governing of Men,* points out that certain needs are common to all of us. When these needs are threatened, we feel stress. These are the basic challenges which create tension in all humans:

- Threats to life and health.
- Loss of means of subsistence whether in the form of money, job, business, or property.
- Deprivation of sexual satisfaction.
- Discomfort from pain, heat, cold, dampness, fatigue, and poor food.
- Enforced idleness.
- Restriction of movements.
- Isolation.
- Threats to children, family, and friends.
- Rejection, dislike, and ridicule from other people.
- Capricious and unpredictable behavior on the part of those in authority on whom one's welfare depends.

While these threats will produce tension in all of us, no two reactions will be completely alike. The magnitude of any individual's reaction and the ease with which he can adjust to the threat will depend on his earlier experiences in life.

When we were children, much of our lives revolved around the relationship with our parents. We achieved satisfaction by carrying out their wishes and living up to their expectations. If we did what we were told, we were praised. This was the emotional payment for performing a job. If we disobeyed, we were punished.

Most adults act in some situations as if the demands were the same as those imposed on us by our parents in childhood. Drs. A. A. McLean and Graham Taylor, noted psychiatric consultants to industry, point out that even as adults we are unconsciously attempting to "get back" at parents who set strict standards for us as children. You may be really saying to an overstrict father, "I'll show you I can do things my way. I'll show you that I can be independent even though I'm wrong."

In the same way, the drives and ambitions to achieve a top position in management may stem from the echo of a parent's voice saying, "Succeed or no one will love you, for there is no room for failure in this world."

Three possible causes of stress

"What Lincoln is supposed to have said of the public is equally true of that which goes on inside Everyman in his dealings with his own unconscious," writes Dr. Lawrence S. Kubie, New York psychiatrist, in his book *Why You Do What You Do*. "We may be able to fool part of ourselves all the time, and all of ourselves some of the time; but we are not able to fool all of ourselves all of the time. This is why we pay so high a price for the unresolved neurotic forces which lie hidden in all of us."

It is not possible to turn back the clock and relive your childhood. However, understanding some of your needs may help to make you less sensitive to their influence. You may not be able to understand all the reasons why you need status or affection, or why one kind of person brings out the best in you while another forces you to show your worst side. However, a little self-knowledge may help you avoid these situations that exacerbate your emotional Achilles heel.

1. REACTION TO SUCCESS

Many executives want promotion — fight for it — but when

they get it, they discover that they haven't achieved the satisfaction they expected.

Psychologists Fritz Redlich and August Hollingshead have demonstrated that often the faster and the higher an executive moves up, the greater the possibility of emotional difficulty. The reasons might lie in the fact that, having compressed his climb to success into a few years, he feels he has paid too high a price for the executive suite. Or, on reaching the top, a man may resent the fact that he has reached the end of the road. Sigmund Freud commented on the possibility of people being licked by success. They feel that they have been struggling up the wrong mountain. Dr. Lawrence Kubie points out that "often success doesn't make friends, and that each success increases the strain of possible failure."

Sociologist Dr. Burleigh Gardner has identified the qualities people think a successful man ought to have. They constitute a picture of a paragon who could not exist. Obviously an executive struggling to live up to all of them is heading for trouble. Take a look at yourself in relation to the requirements Dr. Gardner outlines. The successful executive must:

● Submit to authority without resentment.
● Have strong drives toward material rewards and prestige.
● Possess the ability to bring order out of chaos.
● Be decisive.
● Be active.
● Have a pervasive fear of failure.
● Concentrate on the practical.

Are you trying too hard to live up to all of them? If so, you may be headed for trouble too!

2. MIDDLE AGE DOUBTS

Often as a man approaches his middle forties, he develops an acute consciousness of age.

A University of Rochester study of people between the ages of 10 and 90 found that generalized feelings of anxiety were particularly marked among people in their forties. Once men reached their fifties, their outlook improved. Apparently, men in their forties are particularly conscious that they aren't really young any more, while those in the next age bracket have accepted the fact that they *are* middle aged and adjust to it.

This "late forties anxiety" is particularly common among executives on the upswing. At this stage in their career, they often face the critical job tests which determine whether they have reached their maximum achievement or whether they will move up even higher.

An executive's pressures may produce inner conflict. With each new success the possibility of failure may become more frightening. As General Stilwell once put it, "The higher the monkey climbs, the more his rear is exposed."

Responsibilities create a sense of loneliness and isolation from others. Gone is the easy, friendly, spontaneous, open, office "nice guy." Now there is fear of exposing a management secret. Many top executives hire an industrial psychologist just to have someone to talk to once a month.

Sometimes an executive in his late forties looks back and feels that he has sacrificed too much in his climb to the top. One company president observed, "Unfortunately, the film of childhood does not get run through for a second showing. I missed too much of my children's first experiences; my daughter's first date, my son's first prom, all found me away on business."

3. FEAR OF RETIREMENT

As they approach the time when retirement may be necessary or desirable, some executives begin to fear the loss of their power and control over the environment. An active, efficient, driving man resents the fact that he will be expected to hand over the reins.

To illustrate, a few years ago a small textile manufacturer of my acquaintance sold out to a large corporation that was diversifying. The bigger company dispatched an executive to learn the ropes from the former owner and eventually step into his shoes. Before a year had passed, the corporation executive was asking for another assignment. As he explained it, "The former owner won't let go. Every time I tell him I feel ready to make a decision or take over part of the job, he finds an excuse to postpone it. Actually, he doesn't want to give up any of his power."

In another actual case a company president, selecting a man to groom for succession, chose an executive he knew was incapable. He hoped that when the time came for his retirement, his "successor" would be so lacking that the board of directors would be forced to ask him to continue!

Retirement will seem like much less of a problem if it does not mean the end of all productive activity. By preparing for retirement, one can avoid its devastating effects. Many executives have found a genuine challenge in charitable or civic responsibilities, which can be continued well beyond usual business retirement age. And during a man's working life, such public service has the additional advantage of contributing to company public relations.

How you can control tension effectively

By now you have learned that tension is an essential part of life. As Dr. Selye points out, "No one can live without experiencing some degree of stress . . . Crossing a busy intersection, exposure to a draft, or even sheer joy are enough to activate the body's stress-mechanism to some extent."

But the fact is, tension has some positive values, too. It forces you to think differently — often creatively. It also stimulates new patterns of activity.

The key, then, is not the avoidance of anxiety and tension, but rather the ability to handle it constructively. Here are a dozen suggestions for tension control — not to eliminate anxiety, but to make it your servant.

1. FACE THE THREAT

Fear or avoidance of tension can be more destructive than the tension itself. Tension leads to illness if the individual remains in a conflict situation which he cannot resolve.

Facing the problem and taking constructive action represents the best way to handle the anxiety. Psychologists know from many studies that the more aware the individual is of tension, and the more he struggles with the problem, the less severe any organic illness. Apparently, this is what happens:

THREAT——⟶REPRESSION AVOIDANCE——⟶
FEAR——⟶PHYSICAL SYMPTOMS——⟶
INABILITY to FUNCTION, EVADING RESPONSIBILITY

THREAT——⟶FACING IT——⟶HEALTHY FEAR——⟶
SPECIFIC ACTION——⟶ADJUSTMENT to THREAT

As Caitlin Thomas points out in *A Not So Posthumus Letter to My Daughter*, "Fearful as reality is, it is less fearful than evasions of reality. . . . It is useless to evade reality, because it only makes it more virulent in the end."

If tension creates the feeling of being trapped, it can't go on forever without damage. Everyone needs to feel that there is something he can do about it, that there is an escape hatch to which he has the key. If not, tension becomes destructive.

2. ACCEPT THE INEVITABILITY OF TENSION

None of us can live completely calm and tranquil lives. We all must face tension from time to time, accept it as a part of a vicious cycle, increasing rather than reducing the anxiety.

Suggestion: When pressures begin to mount, try to recall previous problems that you handled well. All of us have met difficult situations in the past with success. A moment of self-reflection recalling the fact that you survived may help you accept and control the present problem.

Also, remember the momentary nature of anxiety and thus prevent it from building into a volcanic eruption. Writes Ben Hecht, "A wise man cannot evade pain or rage, but when they come to him he greets them as visitors and not as permanent relatives. A man who suffers too long or remains too long angry is not at grips with any enemy, but coddling a disease."

3. TAKE FREQUENT PHYSICAL BREAKS

Reasonable exercise is a healthy tension-reliever. Contrary to Chauncey De Pew's advice to friends that the only exercise he gets is "serving as pall bearer at funerals of friends who exercise," modern medical practice recommends regular physical activity. Heart researchers are demonstrating the recovery rate from a first coronary attack is better among men who are not chained to desks than among men who are.

Exercising a little each day is more beneficial than knocking yourself out on the Sunday tennis court after a week behind the desk. Five minutes of touching toes with straight knees, or brisk walking around your office or home, will help.

Remember that much emotional stress may be relieved by almost any physical activity. Shift your briefcase from one hand to the other, stretch your arms and extend your legs while seated, walk briskly to lunch. Activate your muscles. Dr. Paul Dudley White recommends, "If you want to keep healthy, keep moving!"

4. DON'T CHEAT ON SLEEP

"Anyone can carry his burdens, however hard, until nightfall. Anyone can live sweetly, patiently, purely, until the sun goes down," wrote Robert Louis Stevenson. But if we take our problems to bed with us, they are likely to haunt us in our sleep.

Sleep requirements vary widely, but all of us need some. And the kind of sleep that "knits up the ravell'd sleeve of care" requires some preparation.

A hard day's work done well can make you ready for sleep, but you should give yourself time to unwind before you go to bed. Working late or carrying home a load of problems is an invitation to insomnia.

One good rule is to try to do something different in the evening, whether it is working at a hobby, talking or playing with your children, participating in a community activity or simply watching TV. A change of pace will help reduce the accumulated tensions of the day.

In *Painting as a Pastime* Churchill discusses a number of methods for the avoidance of worry and mental strain. He had this to say: "The element which is constant and common to all is Change. Change is the master key. A man can wear out a particular part of his mind by continually using it and tiring it."

Plan your leisure hours as carefully as your job time if you want to get the maximum benefit. Try not to get in a recreational rut. New people, new places, new books, new experiences of many kinds can help make your leisure genuinely profitable both in pleasure and in reduction of tension. However, do not overstimulate your mind so that it cannot rest at bedtime. Few men can build up mental tension and then expect to shut it off with sleep.

5. KNOW YOUR TENSION-TRIGGERS

Tension does not come without warnings.

For some people the sign may be an increase in smoking; for others, too many luncheon cocktails, or two or three nights of disturbed sleep. Know which are the signals in your case. When you spot them, it is time to take it easy. Make a conscious effort to relax by changing the nature of your activity.

You must be aware of what causes your tension, Dr. Howard Rusk points out in an interesting study:

> Recently two San Francisco physicians interested in the relationship between stress and coronary heart disease performed a study on several hundred middle-aged, hard-working men. Pulse counters were attached to the wrists of these men. They were asked to look hourly at the counters and enter the readings in pocket diaries, describing very briefly their activities that hour.
>
> One of the most active men, subjected to great pressure on the job, found to his surprise that his most stressful activity, judged by peaks in his pulse rate, was driving to and from San Francisco from Burlington over the Freeway.

The point of this story is that sometimes tension comes from unexpected sources — not your work. If you make yourself aware of tension from other sources, you can prepare yourself for the ordeal and perhaps avoid the circumstances in order to lessen the damage.

6. STAY WITH YOUR PROBLEM

We can all recognize within ourselves a drive for completion. We like to get things done, finished. When we can't, tension mounts. We feel frustrated, dissatisfied.

In an executive job, you usually have to keep any number of projects going at once. You have interruptions, emergencies, unexpected demands on your time and energy. These things are beyond your control. They add up to tension because they frustrate the fundamental need you share with all human beings to complete what you start.

That's why it is particularly important to impose order on those problems and activities you *can* control. Don't jump back and forth among your tasks any more than you have to. Try to finish a job so that you can forget it and move on to the next task with a feeling of satisfaction. Make it a habit to look back over your day and add up what you accomplished rather than what you had to leave undone.

In one study appropriately labeled "Ulcers in executive monkeys," Dr. Joseph V. Brody, of Walter Reed Army Institute of Research, found that intermittent stress was particularly destructive to the body. He pointed out that stress must be irregular if it is to cause ulcers. "Continuous emotional stress seems to permit a stable adjustment (at least for a while) under which ulcers do not develop. It is tempting to consider the analogy of the vacuum tube or light bulb which seems to last much longer under conditions of continuous current than when it is subjected to frequent heating and cooling."

7. GET AWAY FOR AWHILE

Take it easy!

This doesn't mean to run away from your problems. Retreat is a highly unsatisfactory way to handle frustrations. But there is a difference betwen running away and moving back for a while to get a fresh perspective on your problems. When you are stumped by a situation, it may be wise to turn away for a while to other challenges.

In his biography of Bertrand Russell, Alan Wood says that Russell "came to learn by experience that if he had to write on something difficult, he should think about it as hard as possible for a few hours or days and then give orders, so to speak, that the work is to proceed underground. Months later he would return consciously to the subject, and find that the work had been done."

"Before I discovered the technique," comments Russell, "I used to spend the intervening months worrying because I was making no progress—whereas now I can devote them to other pursuits."

8. CLARIFY YOUR PERSONAL VALUES

The utility of a personal philosophy is that you don't have to rethink each situation as it arises. You know when you must stand firm with no thought of retreat, and when you may yield without sacrificing your standards.

For example, you may decide that no matter what happens you will never maneuver another person out of the way to achieve a promotion. You may decide to remain inflexible on certain moral or ethical issues. It is up to each man to decide the ground on which he will stand firm.

There *are* some situations when it will be wise to give in. Sometimes, even when you're dead right, it will be a lot easier on your mind and body to yield. Not all battles are worth fighting to the bitter end. Selye pointed out, "Fight for the highest attainable aim, but never put up resistance in vain."

9. BLOW OFF STEAM AT SMALL ANNOYANCES

Don't hug small petty annoyances to your bosom. They have a tendency to build up.

The vice-president of one company told me he faced many pressures as the result of a recent merger, but his problems seemed to center around one of his staff men. This man always came into a meeting with his tie off and collar open.

"I recognized it as a small thing," the executive admitted, "but when I was under pressure it always annoyed me. It seemed to show a lack of respect for our meeting. I found myself objecting to many of his ideas, even though I realized I was hacking away because of my petty annoyance. Finally I called him in and mentioned it. Much to my surprise, he took the suggestion to wear his tie and I felt much better."

In most cases a subordinate doesn't mind correcting a petty matter that annoys you. In fact, the health of your overall relationship might be guaranteed by a readiness to mention such mannerisms and annoyances. You can't afford to put the same emotional investment into these petty matters as important problems. Learn to tackle the little things and clear them up quickly. Don't let them fester.

10. SET PRIORITIES

Too many executives find themselves dashing from one activity to another, seldom experiencing the satisfaction of completing a job. Trying to handle too many jobs at once frequently results in dissipated effort and energy, a feeling of frustration because you aren't handling *any* job to the best of your abilities. I have already mentioned this in another context, but I want to emphasize that sometimes the frustration of uncompleted work can lead to body damage. Laboratory animals as well as executives get ulcers when forced to do too much all at once.

Peter Drucker recommends the following to help make your job activities challenging rather than frustrating:

● Decide on a table of priority. Do the most important jobs as thoroughly as possible before moving on to something else.

● At critical times, try to avoid permitting anything to interfere with your work flow.

A special report to the president of your company, an inventory of stock for the heavy selling season; such things should have priority over your usual responsibilities. A closed door and a silent phone will help you to complete the job without tension.

11. WORK OFF PRESSURE

"Just relax" is usually poor advice for an active executive.

It is *sometimes* necessary to take off to the hills and recoup energy, but more often, activity is the better antidote. Sherlock Holmes said to Dr. Watson, "I never remember feeling tired by work, though idleness exhausts me completely."

"Working anger out of your system," points out George S. Stevenson, consultant to the National Association for Mental Health, "will leave you much better prepared to handle your problem intelligently."

The trick is to work off the tension without lashing out at subordinates and family. Pitch into a physical activity that does not require contact with people, like mowing the lawn, carpentry, or just taking a long walk.

12.   CHERISH GRATITUDE

Nietzsche said, "Nothing on earth consumes a man more quickly than the passion of resentment."

One of the best ways to avoid mounting tension is to live so that others want us to prosper because of what we have done for them. There's a tremendous satisfaction that comes from knowing that others have benefited because we have lived, because we have given of ourselves and made ourselves available.

Someone once said of Frank Weil, former president of the USO, that "I am the better and the richer and the wiser for having walked part of the way with this man." Living so that others may feel that way about you is the best and surest guarantee against plaguing anxiety about one's worth.

7.

How to Get
Better Results
When Acting As
Counselor and Coach

What is performance appraisal? Why is it important? What makes it most effective?

If it hasn't already become apparent to you, I want to state clearly that your ability to "get along" with the people you work with—particularly those subordinates on whom you are depending for your success—is essential. That being so, then you must realize that whether you win or lose the support of your subordinates is dependent largely on the way you counsel and coach them—on the way you appraise their performances.

Indeed, performance appraisal, sometimes known as performance review, consists almost entirely of counseling and coaching. Oh sure, you can always check a man's performance to see if he has made or missed his goals. Just look at the record. But suppose, as frequently happens the man winds up far short of his objectives? Do you coax him or reprimand him? What do you say? How do you say it? Or, suppose he goes far beyond his goals? How do you get him to set *next year's* goals a little higher without destroying his initiative?

Make no mistake about it. *The success or failure of any subordinate's performance rests almost entirely upon the individual manager—you, the boss.* The appraisal interview is your instrument.

To put it in more positive words: If you take the appraisal interview as a good opportunity to offer some counsel and advice, to coach your subordinate a little, to offer him some constructive criticism, then he will know where he has failed and where he has succeeded. He'll know how to please you, and he'll know exactly where he stands in your graces. Chances are, he'll work a little harder to make you even happier and to make himself more content.

Another basic point I want to make about performance appraisal is that too many managers believe the appraisal interview is a magic cure for previous errors and omissions. The problem is that formal appraisal interviews, in most companies, occur only once or twice a year. That's too infrequent to be of real value. Many managers fall out of touch with their staff during the interim, and have little or nothing to say when the time comes to say it.

Other managers "save up" their criticisms and approach these formal appraisal interviews with a long list of employees' mistakes; the lists are then delivered in an explosive broadside for their "shock" value. As a manager, you should never reserve your feedback of performance—the praise, the blame, the advice— for a single annual or semi-annual delivery.

The remedy for both of these errors is easy: manage on a daily basis. Give praise or criticism in small doses when it is deserved. At the formal interviews for appraisal of performance, review *total* perfomance and deliver your constructive advice.

Playing the dual role of the appraiser

It takes considerable skill to communicate appraisal in a way that helps the subject. And it's close to impossible to communicate constructively unless you're clear about your goals. You shouldn't ever use the session as an opportunity to "get everything off your chest." Nor should you try to leave him laughing. The goal of appraisal must always be constructive change.

As an appraiser, you actually play a dual role. You must be both a counselor and a coach. As a counselor you should not content yourself with giving advice (which can promptly be brushed off); instead, try to help the subordinate develop realistic attitudes and worthwhile goals that he can successfully achieve through confident decisions. As a coach, you must strive to bring the subordinate's best abilities into play.

As a counselor you must be supportive, suggestive, leading the individual to the threshold of his own self-insight. You must help establish the climate of confidence. As a coach, you must take another role. You must become informative, inspirational, integrating the unique capacities of the individual into a unified effort. Moreover, since you are a leader, you must coach several individuals into working as a team, as a cooperative unit of individuals all playing the same game.

Arthur Daley of the *New York Times* sports staff tells this baseball story, harking back to a past generation. An incident occurred between the Giants' Al Moore and his manager, John McGraw. Moore had just exhibited his spectacular throwing ability for a game-saving play. Beaming, he came to the dugout expecting a torrent of praise from his boss. But McGraw said nothing of the kind.

"Moore," snapped the manager, "you've just joined our team. Otherwise that throw would have cost you $50. You probably think you made a fine throw. You heard the fans cheering. Let me tell you something, young man. If I were to announce that tomorrow afternoon there'd be a throwing exhibition by Al Moore, how many fans do you think would show up? They come here to see the Giants win, not to see Al Moore exercise his arm."

Conducting the interview with tact and purpose

As I have already stated, considerable skill is required if you are to counsel and coach a subordinate effectively in appraising his performance. Here are what I consider the 10 most important things to remember. Some are quite simple; others are, I'll admit, easier to state than implement.

However, I think they are all important. They are based on my own experience in industrial situations and on years of psychological research.

1. LISTEN

The psychologist Carl Rogers once said, "The biggest block to personal communications is one man's inability to listen intelligently, understandingly, and skillfully to another person."

This is perhaps the single most important thing for you to remember in counseling a subordinate: Approach the interview with your ears open and your mouth shut. Your subordinate is bound to be tense and anxious. *Let him talk.* He doesn't get the chance very often.

Listening both connotes and creates acceptance. In an appraisal interview, your subordinate may feel that his ego is on the chopping block. Your willingness to listen gives him a chance to discuss his point of view. This will decrease his hostility, make him more open to suggestions.

Listening to a man talking freely about himself is the surest way to get to know him. This doesn't mean you must believe everything you hear; it does mean that as you continue to listen you will know more and more about his attitudes, his values, even his abilities.

Listening tells your subordinate that you have a constructive interest in his problems, that you might even have some answers. This gives him courage to raise the questions.

Father Theodore Purcell of Loyola University points out that the mark of a successful supervisor is that "he listens." He provides the following illustrations:

Skilled craftsman Terry O'Boyle, very proud of his work, says: "Things are going pretty good in our shop. We have few grievances. And *you can talk to the foreman* . . . The foreman has been right with me. And the former division man would stop and talk anywhere with you."

Semi-skilled grader Covell Pearson, although not satisfied about Negroes' opportunities, says: "It's pretty hard to understand my foreman. He don't talk much. He's Irish. Though white fellows talk with him. *But he'll listen.* He's one of the best foremen we've had in this department."

On the other hand, old-timer Maurice Decker, semi-skilled machine operator, dislikes one of his foremen because of failure to listen (and, incidentally, makes a clear distinction between the foremen and the company): "The company itself, as a corporation, is a wonderful thing. Only some bosses aren't all they should be . . . One of my foremen is pretty good. One is very nervous. He knows it all. And he don't know nothing! 'Why don't you tell me?' says he. But if I try to, *he won't let me tell him.*"

With all these advantages, why isn't listening more popular? Probably because, for most active people, it's hard work! You make up your mind to listen patiently—then one of two things happens. You either drift off on your own affairs, or you listen for a time—until something you hear sets off a reaction. At this point, you interrupt, contradict, argue, explain—and your period of listening is over.

Carl Rogers suggests echoing the other person. For example, your clerk says: "I can't take these new hours." You say: "The new hours bother you?" The clerk will invariably go on to explain why. This method should not be continued to the point of absurdity—but it's well worth a try. The echo approach facilitates listening in two ways: you must listen in order to echo, and the other man has a chance to correct you if you misunderstand him.

2. KNOW THE JOB

The philosopher Alain once said, "The power of a Caesar or an Alexander rested upon the fact that each had a liking for differences and did not expect pear trees to produce plums."

Often we blunder in appraising a man's performance because we have superficial ideas about his job which he does not share—and perhaps may not even be aware of. One man I know was promoted from plant manager to general manager. His idea of the plant manager's job was to be out on the floor most of the time, keeping an eye on operations. This worked out well for him—but the man who succeeded him as plant manager had a different concept. He believed in delegating supervision to the supervisors, in looking constantly for new and improved methods, and in conducting this search from his desk rather than the factory floor.

To the general manager, the new plant manager seemed lazy and ineffective—though actually he achieved smooth operation and cost-cutting improvements. The two men were constantly at loggerheads, because their images of the job were worlds apart.

You know what each of your subordinates is supposed to do. But, unless it's a straight mechanical operation, you may not know the best way for *this particular man* to do it. Is he getting the desired results in a safe and acceptable manner? If so, don't criticize him because his way is different from yours. If he isn't getting results, a change is required—and the first step toward change is to make sure you and your subordinate agree on the essentials of the job.

3. KNOW THE MAN

So much for the job. You must also know the man.

As a coach, you should know your subordinate's special abilities—and help him to apply these abilities to the job. As a counselor trying to motivate improvement, you should understand his needs and values. Some people, for example, are motivated most by challenge and opportunity; others by money; still others by status.

Your subordinate's idea of a status symbol, incidentally, may be quite different from your own. In the restaurant business, one investigator has reported, meat preparation carries higher status than fish preparation, and it's better to slice celery than to peel potatoes. This esoteric information won't matter much to a restaurant customer—but it might make a lot of difference to the restaurant manager.

Here's another fact you should get to know about a subordinate: How far can you trust his ideas? This depends on both his judgment and his thoroughness. One man never proposes an idea without having worked it out completely; you can be sure all the bases are covered. Another man is impulsive. When he makes a suggestion, even though you're under pressure, you must ask certain questions. Is it foolproof? Has he considered the alternatives? Who will follow up on the details?

This doesn't mean the second man may not be useful—even brilliant. It does mean that unless he changes radically, he will always need someone to check on his plans.

So you must know your subordinates, if not intimately, at least well. Some managers are afraid that knowing their subordinates will make them too soft on appraisal. This doesn't follow. You can respect a man's individuality and uniqueness, but still demand that he do his best.

4. EMPHASIZE GROWTH IN PRESENT JOB

As one executive put it: "Too often I get caught in the trap of telling a subordinate that if he would only correct this one fault, he would be great. He then spends all his time dreaming what it will be like when he is great, thus avoiding facing the necessity of changing his fault! I make the mistake of painting him a rosy future, while he directs his energy into unproductive dreams, rather than confronting the reality of the present." This executive has dramatized the need to emphasize growth in the present.

As Alfred North Whitehead, famous mathematician and philosopher, pointed out, "Life is an unbroken process; we inherit the past but *act in the present*. . . . The present is the holy ground."

Contrary to industrial myth, not everybody wants quick promotion. Many men claim that success takes time and effort. It is unfortunate, then, that too often in an appraisal interview, managers stress the prospects of promotion as if this were the only possible road to achievement. One obvious objection to this policy is that no manager can keep all his promises, stated or implied. An unkept promise (or what an employee *considers* an unkept promise) causes smoldering resentment, poor performance, and unnecessary turnover among ambitious employees.

An even stronger objection to emphasis on promotion is that it drains satisfaction from the present job. A man struggling his way up the promotion ladder may never be satisfied as long as there's another rung to climb. Satisfaction and a sense of achievement should stem from an individual's present accomplishments and his sense of making the fullest use of his abilities—not merely from visions of increased status and power at some future date.

5. KNOW THE RACE YOU WANT HIM TO RUN

Movie tycoon L. B. Mayer and his son-in-law owned a horse together. The horse was considered a good prospect to win the Kentucky Derby. While Mayer was out of the country, the son-in-law entered the horse "for practice" in a race a few weeks before the Derby. The horse won that race; but then it lost the Derby. Said Mayer, "He ran the wrong race."

Knute Rockne, the famous Notre Dame coach, enjoyed whipping his team into a frenzy just before each game. One week the Irish played Iowa. Rockne told his team, "Iowa is poisoning our water; they're stealing our plays." Notre Dame murdered Iowa. The following week Notre Dame played Army and lost. Rockne scratched his balding head and exclaimed with insight, "I made the team play the Army game against Iowa. I whipped them up at the wrong time."

The same mistake occurs in the executive arena. In your zeal for motivating and helping your subordinates, you may spur a man on to do something that really doesn't matter. No one on your staff can maintain top speed all the time, so why should you cry "Wolf!" every day? When the wolf really gets to your door, your man will have run out of energy.

A subordinate will especially resent your enforcing requirements that he knows are not genuinely important. Take the question of tardiness. If an employee is doing routine work with regular hours, he should be in on time every morning. But if he has a free-wheeling job that you know takes many of his evenings, and if he's performing that job to your satisfaction, it is senseless to harp on his occasional tardiness. A job isn't a jail sentence. Inspire people to perform—don't make them feel they're doing time.

6. USE CRITICAL INCIDENTS, NOT GENERALITIES

In your counseling discussion with your subordinates, try to drive home your ideas with concrete illustrations.

Glittering generalities won't do the trick. Senator Harry Byrd of Virginia once said, "Let's take the bull by the tail and look the situation in the face!" Such generalities may be fine in politics, but they won't work in business.

In counseling a subordinate you must not become bogged down

in too many details. However, you should be specific about the behavior you consider unsatisfactory. Point out the budgets missed, indicate the details forgotten, or direct attention to the production schedules never met.

An executive cannot live in the patient hope of a subordinate eventually fulfilling his potential. He has to hold the man to the record. "Love," said Santayana, "is very penetrating, but it penetrates to possibilities rather than the facts." You must be aware of the facts and hold a subordinate accountable for the realities.

7. STRESS ACCEPTANCE

A man's errors are rarely fatal. As his boss, you probably feel that some improvement is always possible—and this feeling must be communicated to the individual. You should, therefore, admire his strengths; but point out his weaknesses. Don't condemn them, just help him improve them.

If you have actually given up on a subordinate—if you feel that his work is not satisfactory and that he can't or won't improve sufficiently to hold the job—you will not help him by going through the pretense of an appraisal interview. Stop trying to offer constructive criticism. Tell him frankly that in your opinion his work won't do. Then suggest a transfer to a more appropriate job, if this seems desirable, or fire him.

Remember, a man should *ap*preciate, not *de*preciate, under your guidance. This requires that you criticize a man's performance only when you think there is an opportunity for growth.

8. AGREE ON CHANGES IN HIS BEHAVIOR

If you have a real discussion with your subordinate, rather than a dictation session, you should be able, at the end of the session, to agree on mutual goals—standards for improvement. This means, of course, *genuine* agreement—not just a "yes" wrung out of either party.

The changes you want in your subordinate's behavior can occur only when you and he see the problem in the same way and agree on the means of solving it. Short of agreement, only surface improvements are possible. This, of course, doesn't mean that if your subordinate raises objections to your point of view, you should immediately abandon it. His objections may be unrealistic. You are the manager—and his performance is your responsibility. But you should be open to discussion and willing to change your position if it turns out to be wrong.

Don't let the discussion degenerate into a debate. This is the kind of debate nobody wins.

9. SET UP A TIMETABLE

One of the most important marks of a manager is the way he delegates. A poor manager won't delegate at all. A mediocre manager will delegate wholesale, without adequate controls. A good manager delegates with a timetable. He wants progress reports in time to take positive action when problems begin to crop up.

Almost everyone works better when he has a deadline. We all have a certain amount of inertia; a deadline gives us the pressure we need to conquer inertia. Also, setting a deadline helps us get started on a plan to meet it.

This is especially true of appraisal. When you and your subordinate have reached agreement on a change in the way he is to do his job, the next step is to agree on a date by which the change is to be accomplished. If it's a complicated change (like reorganizing work that involves several people), it may be well to set intermediate deadlines for progress reports.

Setting up a timetable ends the discussion naturally and constructively, with a plan for accomplishment during the coming year.

10. OBSERVE LIMITS

The path to a man's downfall is often paved with his manager's good intentions. As I pointed out in Chapter One, you are not your subordinate's brain surgeon, his minister, or his psychoanalyst. Remember, there are only three fundamental ways to change a man: religious conversion, psychotherapy, and brain surgery. You, as a manager, are not qualified in these three disciplines.

Certain problems are off limits. If he's an alcoholic, for example, there's little point in telling him to "pull himself together." He's probably been trying to do that for years. You can perhaps help him, however, by telling him to get professional treatment or to quit the job.

Also, resist the temptation to cover up his alcoholism or other emotional problems that interfere with performance. You have no way of judging how serious these problems may be, and you do people no favors by hiding or ignoring emotional problems that show up on the job.

"The executive cannot assume the role of the psychiatrist," said Dr. Milton R. Sapirstein, head of the Organizational Psychiatry Division of New York's Mount Sinai Hospital. "Therefore, before confronting a man on a personality problem, the executive should ask himself who the individual is destructive against. The neurotic either directs his hostility inward, on himself, or outward on others. If he's destroying *himself*, it's really none of management's business. If he's destructive to the environment—his colleagues or subordinates—then management not only has the right but the responsibility to step in and try to suggest that the man seek help."

For the top executive, then, the question can be narrowed down to a single distinction. An employee's behavior—no matter how eccentric—becomes management's legitimate concern when, *and only when*, it affects performance on the job, either his own performance or that of others. (See my comments in Chapter One under executive involvement in personal affairs of subordinates.)

One major value of this approach is that it avoids the confusing and misleading assessment of personality traits. In turning the attention to *results*, this approach not only provides a yardstick which management is equipped to use, it puts personal problems into an appropriate framework.

What to do when improvement is doubtful

Appraisal, counseling and coaching, as I have said, is for the employee who has a future with the company. But occasionally you will feel that a man has come to the end of the line. Serious complaints come from subordinates or colleagues. What then?

Management should never *decide* on the basis of these reports. Instead, you should have a hypothesis, and put the theory to the test. Review the facts objectively:

● Has his performance seriously deteriorated compared to his previous record?

● Has his performance deteriorated compared to the *company's* standard? The company's performance?

Assuming that the answers are in the positive, you still have a problem in ascribing causes. Is the employee totally incapable of better performance, or is he being drained by emotional problems? If signs point to the latter, *keep hands off*.

Psychiatrists agree that there is much risk in recommending that a subordinate get therapy. If you do decide to discuss his problem, you are on your safest ground if you discuss the *job*, not the *man*. Actually, that is all you have a right to discuss. If his behavior has affected others in his department, use that as a starting point. If his judgment has been faulty, his performance under par, those are legitimate subjects for discussion.

Of course, if there is no emotional or personal problem involved, and if the man simply is not up to the job, then he must be discharged. Again, stick to the facts. Fire the man on the basis of poor performance, for example, not "poor attitude." (See Chapter One for some additional advice on how to fire a man.)

When to call in the expert

If, during your counseling sessions, you open the door to a discussion of emotional problems and psychiatric help, you will probably be expected to come up with a recommendation. Accordingly, it is often best to have some qualified sources of help lined up in advance.

A physician is handy as a go-between. If you have a company doctor, let him make the recommendation for a family counselor or psychiatric consultation. If the man has a trusted family physician, perhaps he can make the referral.

If you have no such contacts, or are otherwise uncertain of the best local psychiatric services, you may be interested in the facilities offered through the Mount Sinai Hospital in New York. Under federal grant, a pilot project has been developed for psychiatric-industrial cooperation. The hospital's Division for Organizational Psychiatry, headed by the same Dr. Sapirstein I quoted a few pages earlier, has evolved a total mental health package providing care, treatment, and prevention for organizations, industry, and industrial employees. Business and other organizations can arrange for psychiatric services on an annual retainer basis.

"However," you may ask, "what can I do *during the appraisal interview* to help a man who may be adversely affected by outside problems?"

All you can do in talking to your man is discuss the job, not the man; discuss job performance, not attitudes or morals.

I heard one executive tell an honest, well-liked but failing supervisor, "I don't *care* if you stay up all night reading the Bible. All I know is that something is interfering with your performance!" In this case it was alcohol.

The manager, then, must concentrate on job results, refuse to become a psychiatric diagnostician, and offer the man patience as he struggles with his problem.

Most important, this struggle with a disturbed employee should only occur when you have an individual who was previously effective but who is now in trouble, and you hope that with professional assistance he will become again an important human resource.

Benefits and dividends of appraisal

Each company has its own ideas on what aspects of work should be appraised, how they should be rated, and what weight should be given to different factors. Furthermore, not only each company, but each job, each manager, and each subordinate is unique. An executive will get maximum mileage from an appraisal or counseling interview when he understands and respects the differences among men.

An added dividend can also accrue from a well-handled appraisal of a subordinate who has other people reporting to him: If the manager being appraised leaves his boss's office with a feeling that something worthwhile has been accomplished, he will be likely to approach the appraisal of his own subordinates with a healthy and positive attitude. And he can use what he has observed during his appraisal when he is conducting interviews with his own subordinates. This chain reaction can do much to ensure that the appraisal interview will not become a pro forma exercise, dreaded by all concerned, but a vital part of the company's management development program.

8.

How to Motivate
Your Subordinates

You probably would not have gotten this far in your business career if you did not have some basic knowledge about how to deal with and motivate people. For the ability to get people to work *with* you and *for* you—in short, the art of motivating others toward common goals—is essential to the success of any manager.

There are four key words which inevitably crop up in any discussion of the subject of motivation. They are money, fear, goal-setting, and morale. In fact, these words so dominate the subject that they tend to be viewed as "methods." Certainly, they are responsible for many misconceptions.

Just to clear the air, let's look at each before we proceed:

1. *Money.* By and large it is true that if an employee is not paid a fair wage, nothing you do is likely to stimulate him to greater productivity. Unless, of course, jobs are scarce and he is starving. In fact, psychological studies have demonstrated that when an employee feels he is underpaid, he tends to overemphasize the amount of energy he puts into a job.

But that is not the same as saying money is a good motivator across the board. For some people it may be. For others, it ranks low on the scale.

More important, it is unlikely to be the easy answer to *your* motivation problems. Rather than getting caught up in the pros and cons of the money question, you'll want to know what you— as a manager—can do personally.

2. *Fear of punishment* ranks second in the popular tool-kit of basic motivators. The truth is that fear is primarily effective in two instances: (1) as a last resort—"You'd better improve your performance or you'll be looking for another job!" and (2) as an emergency stimulant when short bursts of extra effort are desirable—"You'd better get that work done before the boss returns." But neither of these situations is typical. What you want is a continuing method of dealing with the day-to-day ongoing job.

Fear, incidentally, can have a function over a continuing period so long as it is not fear of a person but *fear of a situation.* That is, fear of the consequences of one's own failure. In such cases, the manager's job may be one of protecting an employee against his own fear lest it completely paralyze him.

The problem with fear as a motivator is that, when fear is used to increase output, it turns to hatred of the feared object-and productivity grows not greater, but deteriorates. In short, the man who is afraid of the consequences that his boss is likely to bring upon him, is as likely to hate the boss as to obey him. But the employee who is afraid of losing his job because of his own incompetence will usually welcome the supervisor's instructions and advice.

3. The third byword that dominates the slick talk about motivation is *goal-setting.* This is closer to the heart of the problem, since goals are a fundamental requirement for getting people to act. I need not go into depth on the reasoning behind production line quotas. However, you must bear in mind that goals are most effective as motivators when they are capable of attainment and when they represent a community interest (when everyone has a stake in reaching the goals).

Let's look at these two considerations for a moment:

Goals have to be set right—neither too high nor too low. *Low goals* that are too easily reached soon lose their excitement. There is no thrill in attainment. *High goals* provide a challenge. The employee's competitive needs are satisfied in beating the record. But the goals should not be set so high that they are beyond reach. Unreasonable goals soon discourage effort.

Psychological experiments demonstrate that after failure to reach goals, employees set standards lower the next time they undertake a job. Failure often results in *present* frustration, and the desire to try harder in the *future* is thus reduced. Here are some basic considerations to keep in mind when you set goals for your people:

● Set a target *above* the present level.

● Keep it within the range of your department's ability to function successfully.

● Make the goal specific. (Not "Let's all try harder," but "Let's aim to reach 5% over last year.")

● Consult your people and let them have a voice in setting the goal. Give their need for self-esteem a chance to overlap with your need for improvement.

A final point on goal-setting: Make sure that the basic objectives or policies are established by management. If you don't set realistic goals for them, then your employees will set their own. On occasions when this has happened, the self-set goals by employees have been neither as high nor as effective as those established by management.

4. Now to *morale*. Most business executives have been brainwashed into believing that morale is some magic touchstone. They attribute too much to morale, high or low, and look upon it as a primary motivating influence.

To be sure, morale has its place. But the truth is, high morale does not always contribute to increased productivity. A happy worker is not necessarily your most productive worker.

The value of high morale is that it pays off in low turnover and less absenteeism among employees. In these respects it does contribute to higher productivity, but only indirectly. Probably the most intangible benefit of high morale is that it provides a better climate for supervision. High morale is a source of emotional comfort for the supervisor. Criticism and instruction are likely to be more effective when morale is high.

So much for the misconceptions regarding financial reward, fear of punishment, goal-setting and morale as factors in motivation. To some extent, these factors may be present in any business situation. They may even be part of the "big picture." But they are beside the point when you ask yourself the question, "What impact can *I* have on my employees?"

Be tough, but not disliked

What about the "little picture?" What can you do, right now, to motivate the people in your department? Plenty. By taking certain measures personally—and by avoiding certain critical pitfalls—you may exert greater motivational stimulus than all of the previous factors combined.

Let me illustrate this by relating an experience. In two major industrial firms where I have conducted attitude surveys among salaried and executive personnel, I have found that if supervisors are tough, hard, demanding, and unreasonable, employees soon become disheartened. On the other hand, if supervisors are really concerned about personal welfare, employees start to exert real effort toward the achievement of corporate goals. This isn't news. This was the basis of the so-called Hawthorne experiments conducted at Western Electric more than 30 years ago, and it set the stage for industrial psychology.

But in both of the companies I studied, I found that there were always a few supervisors about whom the following statements were made: "I wouldn't work for him for *anything*!" "I refuse to go to a meeting with that supervisor because he rips me apart!" "He has only his own interests at heart." "I won't put myself out an extra inch for that guy."

The irony is that, after talking to the supervisors about whom these statements had been made, I concluded that they really didn't match the descriptions. None of them was the kind of narrow-minded, bull-of-the-woods supervisor who would have said, "I'm not going to change. I may be tough, but I don't want them to think I'm a hypocrite, too!"

In each case I was told something like this: "I know I'm tough, I, myself, was raised under a demanding supervisor. I'm concerned about productivity. I believe every man should put in a day's work for a day's pay. If I don't sit on these people they won't get anything done."

One of these tough supervisors asked me to look at the record. He said he had done more for his people than many well-liked supervisors had done for this same department in the past. Working conditions under him were better, more and better equipment was being used, the men's room had been renovated, safety standards were higher, and so forth. I checked with the president, and all that was true.

All the tough supervisors, furthermore, were distraught by the image that they had created among their personnel. They didn't *want* to be disliked, but they were compelled by their own high standards to get the work out despite the inertia of their subordinates. Therefore, when I suggested some methods for motivating their people, they listened and were grateful.

From this, I conclude that a supervisor may be tough and demanding. But if he evidences measures of compassion, if he is counseled about the image he presents to his subordinates, he could be made an even more effective supervisor. I have never met a manager who said, "I'm disliked, and that's the way I want it."

The only way a person can get away with this kind of attitude is if a) he owns the company and holds all the marbles himself; b) he is desensitized to the feelings of others, or c) he overpays his employees so much that they can't afford to quit. William Randolph Hearst, for example, was able to telephone his executives, question them and demand answers in the middle of the night—because they all knew that no one else would pay them double or triple their worth, as Hearst did.

Be "people-conscious"

This important point must be made. To be effective as a manager of people, you must first become sensitive to their image of you, and second, you must be sensitive to their needs as individuals. Finally, you yourself must be capable of change. Your subordinates may require it.

It was originally assumed that a supervisor had an either/or choice. That is, he had to be either "employee-oriented" or "production-oriented." As a supervisor became more employee-oriented (more compassionate and interested in his workers), he became less production-oriented (less mindful of production quotas or quality control). The reverse situation was also thought to be true.

But studies at Ohio State University have shown that both employee and production orientation can be woven together to produce a *more effective* supervisor. In fact, as Robert L. Kahn put it when reviewing these studies, "Most successful supervisors *combine* employee-centered and production-centered orientations, working out their own creative way of synthesizing these two concerns."

I agree with Kahn. I believe both orientations can be blended together to contribute to more effective supervision. The remainder of this chapter will explain how to do this, based on my experiences and observations in business and industrial situations.

Avoid deadly "demotivators"

Your goal as a manager is not to get people to like you. You are not running a popularity contest. But if you can keep people from actively *disliking* you, you will have achieved a fundamental objective.

Put it another way. The goal is not so much doing things to motivate your people, but to keep yourself from doing certain things which *de*motivate them. The latest research has confirmed the long-suspected fact that there are certain negative factors which are so powerful that any one *can cancel every positive thing you do to stimulate and motivate your subordinates.*

The psychologist Herzberg developed a theory that there is a continuum of several factors which, *though they are acceptable* to an individual, do not necessarily motivate him. Yet, if these same factors are *unacceptable* to the individual, they actually become negative motivators. These potential "dissatisfiers," which might preclude the individual from achieving his most effective performance, include such things as salary and salary benefits, beneficent company policies, physical working conditions, and administrative practices.

The theory came to be known as the "Hygiene Theory," and

has been described as advocating a sterile environment in which such viruses as poor salary administration, inadequate working conditions and burdensome administrative practices did not contaminate the organization.

This theory was particularly applicable in the case of highly trained or creative people.

I have a theory that elaborates on Herzberg's concept. Accepting Herzberg, I have observed that there are some additional potential dissatisfiers, any one of which can completely demotivate an individual. A manager can have every personnel factor in his favor. He can have top wages, top morale, realistic goals, experienced and seasoned employees, and everything else—but if he commits one of these cardinal mistakes, he will critically limit his chances of success.

Here are the things you will want to avoid if you are concerned about motivating your people:

1. NEVER BELITTLE A SUBORDINATE

No man likes to think that others regard him as stupid. He may have doubts of his own, but he doesn't like others agreeing with him. Generally you can reprimand an employee using any other term—lax, lazy, indifferent, sloppy—but call him stupid and you will rapidly destroy his initiative. This term flattens most people. After all, how can a man throw himself into his work when he's just been labelled incompetent?

2. NEVER CRITICIZE A SUBORDINATE IN FRONT OF OTHERS

This sounds trite and banal. Everyone knows this is a cardinal sin, but few managers practice it. The temptation is there. The pressure is on. You rush out to your secretary and say, "For God's sake, Marie—can't you *ever* get it straight?" Marie is mortified in front of her girlfriends. She will never forget the insult. Nor will she forgive you for it.

3. NEVER FAIL TO GIVE YOUR SUBORDINATES YOUR UNQUALIFIED ATTENTION, AT LEAST OCCASIONALLY

You don't have to devote every waking moment to your employees. But from time to time it is important to give your undivided attention to every person under your direct control, individually. From time to time, take each person into your office; in privacy, give him your complete attention for a few minutes. Make him think you care about him. Don't let the telephone disturb you, don't let your secretary or anyone else interrupt; if you do, this person will feel that there is probably *no* occasion when he can hold your undivided attention.

4. NEVER ALLOW YOUR SUBORDINATES TO THINK THAT YOU ARE PRIMARILY CONCERNED ABOUT YOUR OWN INTERESTS

Your own future may very well be your primary concern, but try not to communicate this to others. You *don't* want them to think that you are selfish, that you are manipulating them for your own purposes. In other words, don't ask your secretary or your assistant to stay at the office late at night so *you* can impress the vice-president tomorrow. Allow *them* to share the credit. (It wouldn't hurt if you stayed in the office late yourself occasionally, setting an example for others.)

5. NEVER PLAY FAVORITES

This is another cardinal rule of good supervision. When you start to make exceptions because of personal preference—especially when the person you favor is playing up to you—the rest of the staff adopts a "what the hell" attitude. I had an experience that illustrates this point. A supervisor regarded as "autocratic" was accused of playing favorites. He wouldn't let any of the secretaries in his office get away with anything—except for one. He never chastised or criticized this particular secretary even though she was notorious for spending a lot of time making personal telephone calls. His reason was that she frequently stayed at the office late in order to get work done. (Naturally, that was because she wasted so much time during the day.) But the rest of the secretarial staff knew that the supervisor was being manipulated, and resented it. Consequently, the girls became demotivated.

6. NEVER FAIL TO HELP YOUR SUBORDINATES GROW—WHEN THEY ARE DESERVING

Try to be a fighter for your subordinates. The company may be hard put for cash, but your employees must feel that you will try to get raises for them—if, of course, they are deserving. Always inform your people of openings within the company to which they might aspire. Don't try to hold back a good man, even if it means transfer out of your department into another. (By holding him back, you will probably lose him anyway when he quits to seek another job.) Make your employees feel that you will go to bat for them.

7. NEVER BE INSENSITIVE TO SMALL THINGS

Never make loose or rash statements. You'll regret it. Here's an extreme example: A supervisor in a company of my acquaintance already had a terrible reputation among his department's employees. To top it off, one day he roared in a fit of temper, "I don't care how long you've been in this firm. Seniority means nothing in my department." This company had been without a union for 75 years, but with this crack in management's armor, the union finally gained admittance. Its organizing propaganda theme: "Seniority means nothing."

An executive of a men's jewelry company asked me about a job offer he had received. It offered him more money and somewhat greater responsibility. I let him talk. Finally, he said, "I can't leave my company; the president is tough and demanding, but he is considerate in ways I will never forget. When my wife and I went back to Paris and checked into our hotel, there was a tremendous bouquet of flowers from the president and his wife. He had remembered that this was where we had honeymooned."

8. NEVER "SHOW UP" EMPLOYEES

It's embarrassing to an employee to have his boss show off at his expense—for example, by doing a particular job better or faster than the employee can do it himself. Of course, most bosses can—that's why they've risen. But it is important to a man's dignity to be able to do *something* well on his own, and when you take his work away, you also take his self-respect. You are, in short, demotivating him. If you find that you must take his work away often, don't embarrass him; discharge him and get someone else to do the job as you want it done.

9. NEVER LOWER YOUR PERSONAL STANDARDS

Tolerating the efforts of weak or inefficient personnel utterly destroys the initiative of the best men in your company. Here's why, in a succint statement published by the Research Institute of America:

> The mediocrity of colleagues can muzzle the initiative of the dynamic doer who has high standards for his own performance—especially when the "mediocres" are permitted to stand on the sidelines and throw darts at new ideas. Management often tolerates a certain percentage of people whom they have given up on—men who will never pull their own weight. But if these people are permitted to remain in key positions, just the simple fact of their presence can cost the company the loss of an endless chain of worthwhile people who don't have to work against such odds. And, incidentally, whether they remain on the payroll or leave for greener fields, you've lost a man if he has decided it doesn't pay to knock himself out.

10. NEVER VACILLATE IN MAKING A DECISION

It is a sign of strength in supervision and management to be able to make decisions promptly and wisely. If you lack confidence, if you are afraid to "stick your neck out," then your employees will also lack confidence and be demotivated. Add vacillation in decision-making to any of the previous nine "critical negatives," and your whole motivation program will crumble around you. This is the last straw.

Of these 10 negative points, you will rarely find more than one or two in any single manager. A man who makes a practice of violating these principles regularly simply isn't going to remain in management—unless, as was previously mentioned, he has complete control of the company. Even then, you won't find him violating all 10 negatives. It is, as always, a matter of degree.

Eighteen ways to insure positive motivation

I have never subscribed to the belief that work is a curse put upon man by God because Adam and Eve ate the apple. That's a

distortion of reality. There is enough evidence—in fact, it abounds
—that man *needs* to work. He needs to compete and to stretch
himself.

Songwriter Cole Porter provides a good example of this need.
In 1937 he was severely injured when he fell off a horse and both
his legs were crushed. This led to long years of pain and more
than 30 operations. Meanwhile, Porter immersed himself in his
work. His best songs were written in the 10 years following the
accident.

When asked by a reporter if he composed easily, Porter replied,
"When this horse fell on me I was too stunned to be conscious of
great pain, but until help came, I worked on the lyrics of the
songs for 'You Never Know.'" Porter, feeling this tremendous
desire to work, kept his mind busy even in time of great physical
agony.

This anecdote suggests that, to a great extent, man is inherently
motivated. Man *must* work. That is why I think if you avoid com-
mitting any of the "critical negatives" just discussed, *you will in
many cases give a man a good start toward motivating himself.*

Dr. Douglas McGregor, professor of industrial management at
M.I.T. and former president of Antioch College, elaborates on this
point: "The motivation, the potential for development, the capacity for assuming responsibility . . . are all present in people," he
wrote in 1960. "It is the responsibility of management to make it
possible for people to recognize and develop these human characteristics for themselves."

Another important psychological element in motivating people
is that it is very difficult to motivate large groups of people. It is
relatively easy to motivate individuals.

Therefore, you should concentrate your motivational efforts on
those individual subordinates who have the ability and the know-
how to influence the others. Go beyond titles. Find out who the
influential people are beneath you, the molders of group opinion
within their cliques and spheres of activity. These are the people
who count; they can make your job a lot easier. By setting the
pace, they will also be helping you to motivate others.

So far, we have been concentrating on the *negatives*, the pitfalls
to avoid. But motivating top performance requires *positive* actions
too.

Here are 18 positive suggestions for improving your own capacity to motivate your subordinates. Each one should be integrated into your day-to-day behavior. They are not one-shot cure-alls, but taken as a whole, they add up to effective management:

1. KNOW YOUR STANDARDS, COMMUNICATE THEM,
   AND BE CONSISTENT

When an individual knows he is being evaluated according to a single, fair standard, he has a target to shoot for. He can modify his performance accordingly and try to meet that standard. If your standards are multiple, unfair, or erratic, then employees will try to beat the game. The very *least* that fair standards will do is minimize misdirected efforts. However, standards usually also tell your people just what is expected of them. No one wants to work without an objective.

Part of a standard's effectiveness comes in its consistency. For example, say a company's board of directors looks at an embarrassing profit and loss statement and directs that 10 per cent of all employees be laid off in order to cut expenses. Then six months later, the board demands to know why the company doesn't have any promotable people. The reason is because the board has switched signals. Where do the company's officers stand? The standard against which they were being measured has been changed. People who could have been trained for positions of responsibility were laid off!

Of course, there is nothing wrong with being *flexible* in your standards. To be consistent to the point of inflexibility is poor management. As Ralph Waldo Emerson has said, complete consistency is the hobgoblin of small minds. But if you are going to modify your standards, at least communicate this in advance so that your people can expect a measure of flexibility and remain flexible themselves.

2. BE AWARE OF YOUR OWN BIASES AND PREJUDICES TOWARDS
   PEOPLE SO THAT THEY DO NOT INTERFERE WITH YOUR
   EVALUATION OF PERFORMANCES

All of us have biases and prejudices; no one is completely devoid of them. The question is, are you *aware* of your prejudices? If, for example, an executive is very unhappy with his plant manager because the manager is always five minutes late to meetings, this annoyance may develop into a prejudice. The executive is likely to grade the manager on the basis of his ability to get to a meeting on time, rather than on his ability to manage a plant. A matter of little consequence is interfering with the executive's ability to appraise performance fairly.

How do you become aware of your prejudices? Keep records of your predictions about peoples' performances. If you predict a man's performance, and it doesn't measure up to what you predicted, ask yourself if you aren't responding to some irrelevant variable, such as his religion, his wife, his dirty fingernails, or his untidy desk. If you do have prejudices, your people will perceive them and know you as a supervisor who is not really fair—a man who is responding to his own opinions rather than fact.

3. LET PEOPLE KNOW WHERE THEY STAND

Do this consistently, by means of performance review or other methods. The positives and negatives that are nestling in the back of your head do your people no service unless they know what you are thinking. Give each man sufficient attention; let him be aware that you are looking for ways to help him improve himself. Manifest your concern.

One executive told me in dismay, "The only guy here who really knows what I'm doing and how well I'm doing it, is too busy to tell me." Hence, that executive is demotivated. Anyone else can pat him on the back, but no one else is knowledgeable enough to be sincere about it.

4. GIVE PRAISE WHEN IT IS APPROPRIATE

You should avoid praising every little thing your employees do, for it will quickly lose meaning and may even demotivate them. Moreover, try not to exaggerate in your praise. Praise is like seasoning—a little bit is better than a lot.

Properly handled, praise is one of the best motivating factors. It's especially helpful when you praise someone in the area of his anxiety—where he is trying to do a good job and where you know he feels he ought to be making some progress. It's also a good idea to save your praise for a particularly difficult job, handled well.

It is not, contrary to what you may have been told, a good idea to always give your praise in public. This has pitfalls. If you over-praise a man by just a little, this man may be embarrassed in front of his colleagues and work-fellows. If you underpraise a man in the same situation, it may create doubts in the minds of his work-fellows. So, as a general rule, praise a man in public only if it is important that others know you have a high opinion of him. This, too, might be embarrassing, but it would be even more embarrassing if you didn't praise him at all.

5. KEEP YOUR EMPLOYEES INFORMED OF CHANGES WHICH MAY AFFECT THEM

You don't have to tell every company secret, but it is an evidence of your regard to inform employees of matters in which they have a direct interest. It's another way of showing your concern.

For example, if changes in the corporate structure create a position for which one of your men qualifies, tell him about it. Even though he may not get the job, at least you have given him a crack at it. Avoid the indictment of ignoring your employees' promotional opportunities.

6. CARE ABOUT YOUR EMPLOYEES

You must be sufficiently attuned to the fact that each one of your people is individually concerned about his own future and his own self, and everyone must feel that you, too, are concerned about them as individuals.

Lack of communicating with employees about themselves, lack of caring about them as individuals, is summed up neatly in this poem by Phyllis McGinley: "Sticks and stones can break the bones, when thrown with accurate art. Words can sting like anything, but silence breaks the heart."

The man who best motivates others recognizes that others have purposes of their own that do not necessarily coincide with those of the supervisor or the company. The best supervisors generally help their key employees set their own goals. Many executives think they "care" about employees because they help people do better jobs. Yet, the real test is not merely helping a man carry out *your* purpose; are you willing to help him achieve *his* purpose too?

7. PERCEIVE PEOPLE AS ENDS, NOT MEANS

The object here is to avoid the charge that you are "using" people for your own selfish purposes. The conductor of an orchestra regards his players as individuals, with individual goals, but all working toward a common purpose.

When the explorer Thomas Cook discovered a new island, he named the discovery after the first man who spotted it. He regarded every man in his crew, even the ship's boy, as a partner in the adventure. Cook apparently was a modest man, but his crew loved him for the feeling of usefulness that he gave them as individuals.

8. GO OUT OF YOUR WAY TO HELP

If you are a good manager, you will go out of your way to help others—especially when it calls for only a little extra effort on your part. You *really* help your personnel when you are willing to take pains for them, when you are ready to sacrifice some of your own comfort for them, when you are ready to inconvenience yourself for them.

This means more than merely doing favors for your people. Frequently, it may mean criticizing the person you care about and want to help. Remember, however, that in (a) correcting, where there is an error, (b) improving, where there is deficiency, and (c) strengthening, where there is weakness, you must first know the individual. You must know what gives him joy and what brings him sorrow. And this may take long hours of hard thought to discover.

9. TAKE RESPONSIBILITY FOR OTHERS

If you wish to motivate people, then you must assume some responsibility for what happens to them. This is all a part of caring for your personnel. The supervisor who is concerned has a personal involvement in the success of the subordinate. If the worker fails, then a part of the supervisor also fails. Caring usually creates a bond of responsibility between superior and subordinate.

Famed Frank Stanton of the Columbia Broadcasting System is

known to his men as a leader who cares. When working with a subordinate, he frequently challenges the man with this question: "Is this the best job *you and I* can do together?" The way the question is phrased shows the subordinate that, first, Stanton assumes partial responsibility for the success of the project, and, second, that Stanton cares.

10. BUILD INDEPENDENCE

Again, this is closely allied to caring for your employees. A superior who cares seeks to loosen and ultimately drop the reins of supervision. He would prefer that his subordinates learn to think and act properly, independent of supervision. He wants to give underlings their head. He encourages them to show initiative, to think critically, to ask penetrating questions about their own work.

In short, one of the best ways to motivate people is to help them achieve their own fullest potential through independence.

11. EXHIBIT PERSONAL DILIGENCE

I have never seen a successful supervisor or executive—a man who could motivate the people beneath him—who himself was not highly motivated. The best motivators of men are those who themselves are hard working, almost to the point of total commitment to their work.

You motivate by example. In spite of the hostility behind statements that employees make about hardworking, dedicated superiors, there is always a feeling of pride as well. Employees like to feel that they are living up to an image of their boss, particularly when the boss is devoted to the job of making his company successful. And, conversely, the best way to demotivate an employee is to stop working, yourself.

12. BE TACTFUL WITH YOUR EMPLOYEES

Tact covers many things: consideration, courtesy, a sense of balance, an appreciation of the views and feelings of others. It's important in dealing with any employee, but critical in dealing with women. One of the best ways to learn how to be tactful is to observe those whom you yourself consider tactful, polite, diplomatic. Listen to their conversations with others, observe their behavior, try to find out how they handle themselves in arguments and uncomfortable situations.

It has been said of Thomas Jefferson, who always made others feel at ease, "He never sought to overshadow or overawe. Inferior men were never embarrassed or depressed in his presence. He was amazingly thoughtful and considerate."

13. BE WILLING TO LEARN FROM OTHERS

As a manager, it must be assumed that you know a great deal about the work of your department and personnel. But be honest with yourself. Acknowledge that you may not have all the information and new knowledge that could be helpful to you and your people. When others come to you with an idea, a suggestion, a proposed change, give them an honest audience. At least, *listen* to what they have to say.

You may not like the idea; you may have positive proof that the idea absolutely will not work. But, by lending an ear, you will motivate employees into thinking for themselves—and you may learn a thing or two yourself, which, when applied for practical purpose, will further motivate the originator.

This is one of the basic reasons for the regular success of "beneficial suggestion plans" used in industrial plants and factories. Employees like to show off their insight and intelligence to their bosses; and the best bosses like to learn from their employees.

14. STAY FLEXIBLE

Don't have hard and fast regulations and policies, or procedures and plans that never sway even under the most extreme pressures. Stay loose. Be sensitive to the possibility of change, especially when the ideas or pressures rise from below.

Winston Churchill appreciated that it was not a sign of weakness to modify an opinion or a position. "There is nothing wrong in change," he said, "if it is in the right direction. To improve is to change, so to be perfect is to have changed often."

15. DEMONSTRATE CONFIDENCE

If you have any doubts about your department, your staff, your projects, or your company, review them alone and in private. Exhibiting doubt to subordinates disheartens them and completely destroys any motivation. If the leader is afraid, what is there left to inspire in followers?

Conversely, the demonstration of a leader's confidence builds up confidence among others. Show by your behavior and speech that you are confident that the work can be done; that you are confident of your own responsibility and confident of your employees' ability to handle the job.

I recall sitting on a fishing yacht and discussing this subject with a successful company president. He pointed out at the water and said:

> See that school of fish out there? There's one in front, big and strong, and all the others are following calmly and peacefully. If I wound that leader, all the others will either scatter individually or try to devour the wounded one.
>
> I'm like the lead fish. As an executive, I must be big and strong, demonstrating confidence and satisfaction. In this way, all my executives will be motivated to follow me. But if I lose my confidence and exhibit doubt, then all my executives will similarly lose confidence.

16. ALLOW FREEDOM OF EXPRESSION

Assuming that your subordinates are reasonably competent, it never hurts to relax your vigil and allow them to do things *their* way once in a while. Every employee ought to have the right to make his own job more interesting by doing it his own way. All you have to do is be sure that the results are what you seek and that the employee is working within the framework of company policy.

Countless experiments have shown that, even on assembly line operations, this technique works. Girls who are given some discretion and choice as to what time to take their coffee breaks, are more highly motivated than when the coffee break times are simply posted. A salesman who schedules his road trips himself is likely to work harder, see more customers in less time, than when he receives a schedule from the home office. The psychologist sees in this phenomenon the individual's urge for independent action and the need to demonstrate his competence.

17. DELEGATE, DELEGATE, DELEGATE

Assuming that the people who work for you are competent individuals who want to get ahead, delegate to them as much of your burden as possible. Pressure often motivates employees. Let them bite off as much as they can chew; then, let them ride with their own decisions (insofar as possible), let them learn through their own mistakes, and let them revel in their own successes.

By so doing, you not only motivate competent men, you also build people you can rely upon when the going gets tough. Paul Meyer, president of the Success Motivation Institute, was quoted on this subject in *Business Management* magazine: "Give your man a project and the freedom to do with it as he wants. Make sure he can either break it or make it on his own. Meanwhile, protect yourself by making sure the project is in an area of his interest. Chances are, the man will work like the devil to make the project 'go.'"

Joe Crail, president of Coast Federal Savings and Loan, strives to delegate responsibility to his executives. And to make sure that they bear the responsibility well, he makes them share the risks. Like all good executives, Crail knows that the higher a man climbs in management, the more he must be held responsible for his own decisions.

Crail, for example, has set up a strict policy on when and when not to grant loans to applicants. If one of his staff recommends an exception to policy, Crail says, "O.K. But you will have to share the risk. I don't want you to play games with my marbles alone. If the loan is forfeited, you pay half and I'll pay half. If the loan is repaid, you collect all the interest." Crail reports that only two men have taken him up on this proposition. One man is now Crail's chief assistant, and the other is now president of a rival bank!

18. ENCOURAGE INGENUITY

This technique works with anyone. In Chapter 11, when I discuss creativity, you will learn that anyone—even the lowest paid clerk—can be creative. You should encourage this creativity and ingenuity by challenging your subordinates to beat your system of doing things. If, for example, your filing system is not satisfactory, don't change it yourself; have your clerks and office manager recommend changes.

Paul Meyer of the Success Motivation Institute knows the value of this technique and suggests it to his clients. He tells a story to illustrate how he challenges his own office staff in this manner: A typist questioned a tax report that Meyer had prepared. He challenged her to prove her point. That evening, she asked an accountant to look it over. He gave her an idea that she carried to Meyer, who used it the next day to save nearly $3,000.

An exception to the rules

I have just given you 18 suggestions for improving your technique of motivating subordinates. Earlier, I listed 10 things *never* to do for fear of demotivating people. Now, I am going to pull the rug out from under everything I've said.

There may be a few people in your company to whom none of the above rules apply. Count yourself lucky if your department has just one or two. These people are rare. They are the "comers" —the fast-rising young executives with the burning desire for success and the talent to get it. They are your firm's most valuable asset, for a comer thrives on challenge and finds in his work much satisfaction and personal achievement. He literally works himself to death.

This kind of person needs no push from anyone—especially from his immediate supervisor. The best way to manage him is *not* to apply the rules we discussed. On the contrary, your best course is simply to *get out of his way*. Leave doors open for him, let him move on through, let him know what goals you have in mind, reward him when he gets there, and tell top management that you've got a tiger by the tail.

And, as the Research Institute of America cautions, "don't rain on his parade." Don't spoil his initiative with over-management. He doesn't need you; you need him. General Ira C. Eaker tells the story of how he first met Curtis LeMay, who later became Air Force Chief of Staff. In 1937, as a young lieutenant, LeMay was introduced to Eaker as the navigator who would lead a flight of aircraft on an important mission to South America.

Eaker happened to wonder out loud how such an important

mission could be entrusted to such a young lieutenant. The answer: "Because LeMay happens to be the best damned navigator in the Army Air Corps."

Someone had spotted LeMay as a comer.

In conclusion, remember that all these suggestions for motivating people are ones that you, as a boss, can implement within your own sphere of activity. You may not be able to control the working conditions or the general wage scale or many other motivational considerations.

But when it comes to controlling and motivating the *people* who work directly under your leadership, then the suggestions presented here can be of immediate and immense value. The degree of their motivation will be reflected in the quality of their work, and the quality of their work will reflect upon you and your value to the company.

9

Getting Others
To See Things
Your Way

Have you ever tried to persuade a supervisor to transfer to another division?

What about the boss? Have you ever tried to talk him into modifying a plan to which he had previously committed himself?

Have you ever tried to talk up a "great new program," one that met with only lukewarm acceptance?

If so, then you will probably agree that every businessman has a great need for the ability to persuade people. The man who gets ahead—and stays ahead—is the fellow who has the talent of getting others to see things his way, to convince others to take action along the lines he recommends.

Harry S. Truman once said that when he was President, one of his principal activities was "to bring people in and try to persuade them to do what they ought to be doing anyway, without persuasion. That's what I spent most of my time doing."

The trick, of course, is to get people to see it your way *will-*

ingly. When you have to resort to commands and orders, you may encounter solid resistance.

Brainwashing and threats

There is no easy road to effective persuasion. There is no simple mechanism, no easy guideline, no verbal bag of tricks which you can employ to persuade another human being to take action along a particular course. There *are* some sure-fire techniques, but they are not within the democratic process.

For example, there is the technique known as brainwashing. The Russians make great strides when they "persuade" people. Their technique is merely to isolate the victim from all stimuli (by confining him to a bare room or isolation booth) and feeding him only those ideas they want him to retain. It has been proved that in a relatively short time, even a normal, healthy mind will crack. The fascinating aspect of this technique is that no physical coercion is involved; it is all mental. And that's why it is called brainwashing.

You could persuade a man in your employ by following the same, fundamental principle. For instance, if you'd like a particular employee to resign, merely isolate him from all stimuli. Don't invite him to meetings, cut him off from all memos that are going to people at his level, don't invite him to lunch, don't speak when you pass his desk, don't route mail to him, etc. Eventually, he will get the message and quit.

However, this is manipulative and undemocratic.

Another somewhat crude technique of persuasion is the threat. Threatening a person in order to have him perform in the desired manner is easy—but it may backfire or cause the individual to build up resentment against you. This will make it much more difficult to persuade him to your view the next time you try.

Also, a threat may be *totally* ineffective, depending on the individual. People have several ways of reacting to threats. Among them:

1. "I don't believe that his forecast of doom will actually happen. It's improbable; he's exaggerating."
2. "It can't happen to *me*."

3. "So what? It won't be so bad."
4. "I'm not afraid. Even if the worst comes true, it won't bother me."

In this chapter we are not concerned with threats, fear, and brainwashing as techniques of persuasion; nor are we concerned with the inspirational speech, nor blackmail, nor any other form of manipulation. The lessons you learn in this chapter will be how to employ that kind of persuasion by which the individual exercises some *voluntary* control over his reaction, with positive results. This is the type of persuasion by which you retain the employee's enthusiasm for his job. It is hard work, but it brings results. You will learn how to persuade and still maintain a lasting relationship.

Why it is difficult to persuade others

The fundamental objective of persuasion is to modify an attitude, to change a man's predisposition to behave in a certain manner. Some background information on attitudes will be helpful in learning how to use the principles of persuasion.

If a man has a positive attitude toward his work, it means he is predisposed to work rather than to play golf. If he has a positive attitude toward a minority group, it means he is more likely to consider a person of that group favorably than unfavorably.

However, while attitudes are predispositions toward behavior, they are not *guarantees*. Attitudes merely *influence* behavior. People can be persuaded to change both their attitudes and the consequent behavior.

Why are attitudes important? Why are they so difficult to change? Here are three reasons:

1. ATTITUDES ACCENTUATE CERTAIN ASPECTS OF YOUR ENVIRONMENT

If you have a strongly favorable attitude toward religion, for example, it will tend to stimulate your interest in many things around you that you think are related to religion. You may regard certain occurrences as religious signs, certain items as religious symbols.

An acquaintance of mine is an executive in a company that

manufactures buttons. His attitude toward buttons is positively accentuated. When he mets someone wearing clothes that bear his buttons, those buttons suddenly become more important than the suit. He spots the buttons almost before he recognizes the individual!

2. ATTITUDES SIMPLIFY LIFE

If you have a positive attitude toward professors, you don't have to ask yourself of every teacher you meet, "I wonder if I like this professor?" You have a predisposition toward all teachers; when you meet them, they already have something in their favor. On the other hand, if you have a negative attitude toward a minority group, every man of that group already has one strike against him.

Attitudes simplify things so that your mind is already made up, and not easily changed. That's why psychologists refer to attitudes as "sets." The problem is that you may not be aware of your sets. You should be made more conscious of both positive and negative sets so that they do not interfere with your objectivity.

3. ONCE A MAN HAS AN ATTITUDE, HE WILL DO EVERYTHING POSSIBLE TO RATIONALIZE

A man will go to great lengths to prove himself right, finding reasons that *never before existed* in order to support his own opinion. Once you make a decision to buy a particular make of car, you begin to find all kinds of nonsensical reasons for making your decision. You read all the ads proclaiming the virtues of "your car." Everyone on the road is driving a car "just like yours."

In such cases, you have lost your objectivity. You have increased your resistance to change and reduced your dissonance—reduced your ability to believe in those opinions that do not support your own. You say to yourself, "I haven't changed; the world has changed. *Everybody* seems to be buying the same car I bought."

All of these factors contribute to the difficulty of modifying attitudes. You must be aware that sometimes attitudes can distort the world in your eyes.

Yet, attitudes are important to life. They have their place.

Attitudes are prisms through which the world is filtered into your thinking. They help you focus on the world. They help you make sense out of reality. Without attitudes, the world would be a whizzing, buzzing mass of confusion.

Opinions are the result of attitudes. An opinion is the specific expression of favor or disfavor, reflecting the person's attitude and predisposition in a given set of circumstances.

Appealing to individuals and groups

The literature of psychology reveals that, generally speaking, an attitude can be changed only when one of two conditions prevails: either the attitude and the activities related to it no longer provide the satisfactions previously achieved, or the individual's level of aspiration has been raised.

For example, the psychologist Daniel Katz has pointed out that attitudes toward political parties and voting behavior are difficult to change if there is no widespread dissatisfaction with economic conditions and international relations. As for the attitude changing as per the level of aspiration, take an example common to many companies: A factory hand becomes a supervisor, or a supervisor becomes a manager; in such instances, a man's attitude toward labor unions might change drastically. He is in a new role; the level of his aspirations has been raised.

Until recently, it was thought that the best way to persuade a man to change an attitude was to be either highly emotional, almost overpowering, or to appeal to him through pure logic and presentation of the facts. Psychologists now believe that neither technique will work to the exclusion of the other. Both are relevant.

The most effective persuaders, research shows, are those who appeal to both the intellect *and* emotions of their listeners. They have learned that the more intelligent a person, the more effective an argument based primarily on fact and logic. The less intelligent an individual, the more effective an argument based primarily on emotional appeal.

The reasoning behind this is that more intelligent people can draw their own conclusions and don't require that implications be pointed out to them, as is the case with less intelligent people. However, my advice is that if the issues are complex, it never

hurts to draw the conclusions and implications clearly no matter
how intelligent your audience.

Incidentally—and I throw this in only as a side comment—
it helps to know which people are easily persuaded (those on
whom you might use an emotional appeal to get quick agreement). The following characteristics of personality generally indicate a man who is quickly convinced: passive, shy, inhibited,
withdrawn, dependent, acquiescent; has low esteem of himself;
has much fear of social disapproval; has feeling of personal in-
adequacy.

Influencing group behavior

Let us review, briefly, some of the fundamental principles of
persuasion. These are principles that you probably have already
mastered, but they should be mentioned in passing lest they be
forgotten. Dr. Mark Silber, staff psychologist for The Upjohn
Company, summarizes these principles as follows:

First, in a situation where you want to persuade a group to
follow your lead, never attack the group. Single out the leader,
if you can identify him, and concentrate on his attitude. If you
win him, he will help you influence the others. And winning this
one man will be far easier for you than trying to win a dozen
men who, in their unity, find strength.

Second, keep in mind that you can use the rest of the group
to your advantage in working on the leader. Collect opinions
and ideas from the group. Perhaps the individuals never had a
chance to express themselves. You might suggest that the leader
collect opinions or facts from individuals, then funnel them to
you. This accomplishes two things. It preserves the leader's
dignity, and it alerts the group to the fact that a change may
be forthcoming.

In persuasion never forget that the man who contributes to a
final judgment will work hard to make the judgment a good one.

How to get others to see things your way

1. RECOGNIZE INDIVIDUAL DIFFERENCES

Do you know what stimulates your most important subordinate? What makes him tick? Do you know what kinds of pro-

posals leave your employees cold? Which proposals stir them up and bring them to life?

Whenever you advance an idea, a plan, a proposal, or a program and want to see it adopted, take into account the individuality of the people who compose your audience. Take into account what kind of man you're dealing with. Does he like a summary first and then the details? Or, the details first? Does he like a folksy approach or a sophisticated explanation?

Also consider group identifications. What is the background of your audience? Is the group oriented toward a certain kind of behavior?

In one famous psychological study, in an actual industrial situation it was demonstrated that a financial incentive program designed for all female employees would not work because of group identifications. The extra money was a terrific incentive for girls of Norwegian descent because in their families, they were permitted to spend their own money. But for girls of Italian descent, money was not the right incentive. These girls, by family tradition, were required to throw their money into family funds from which they drew allowances—no matter how heavy their contributions, no matter how hard they worked.

Bear in mind the democratic process. In weighing individuality, is it possible to give your people a choice? Whenever there is an option and people are given the opportunity to choose according to their individuality, chances of winning their support are excellent.

This matter of individual differences is basic to the whole subject of persuasion. In many respects it is basic to life.

Lawrence Appley, president of the American Management Association, often points out that there are four kinds of people in the world:

- Those who *make* things happen.
- Those to *whom* things happen.
- Those who *watch* things happen.
- Those who don't even *know* that things are happening.

You *must* predetermine which kind of person you're dealing with.

A story to illustrate: Gladstone and Disraeli, who were bitter political opponents in Parliament, at various times both served as prime ministers to Queen Victoria. However, everyone knew that the Queen favored Disraeli over Gladstone. When Disraeli was asked to explain why, he said, "Gladstone speaks to the Queen as if she were a public institution. I treat her as a woman."

2. SELL, DON'T DEBATE

Watch good salesmen operate. Study some examples of good advertising. Do you see any debates in these forms of selling? If you do, then chances are the sales pitch isn't too effective.

When you attempt to persuade someone, you are performing the same kind of sales activity as if you were selling vacuum cleaners or cosmetics. The only difference is that you are selling an attitude instead of a product or service. The basic principles of selling can be applied with good results.

In fact, when it comes to persuasion, you might even improve on the standard sales technique. Whereas top salesmen prefer never to mention the competition, and are successful, psychological research shows that in persuasion, you stand to gain by using the competition.

You "use the competition" by anticipating opinions and reactions that are contrary to yours. Typically, you would anticipate a negative reaction to your proposal, then answer it fast and proceed to make a strong case for yourself.

Studies show that if you present only your side of the case, you have not really sold it. That's because when your audience hears the other side of the story it will be more easily "unconvinced" than if it had heard both sides originally. In other words, if you think that your audience originally heard, knows of, or will eventually hear arguments against you, it will pay you to devote some time to the opposition. Give your audience some mental ammunition with which to defend the position you hope it will take.

It will also pay you to anticipate the opposition if your audience is intelligent and sophisticated enough to look for flaws in your argument. Moreover, if you don't *impress* an intelligent audience by your knowledge of the competition, the audience may lose its respect for you and your case. You have to beat your audience to its own best punch.

The one-sided argument works better when the audience is relatively uneducated and unsophisticated. Don't create doubts where none will ever exist.

Always open with the positive story. Moreover, research by the late Dr. Carl Hovland at Yale pointed out the need to present the positive idea briefly. If people seem to buy it without objections, consider stopping immediately. People sometimes freeze after the initial presentation, and the first idea presented often has greater impact than all the concepts which follow.

If the audience seems attentive but not overly responsive, next, outline the opposition's arguments. Don't make a strong case, just mention enough of the negatives to alert your audience to their existence. The purpose is to insulate your audience against having the idea penetrate from another source.

Then, marshall all the facts in favor of your approach. Present all the reasons why you are in favor of the idea. Give this the greatest emphasis.

One final suggestion: Never identify an individual in your audience as a member of the opposition. This often makes him more resistant; he becomes intransigent and you will make a sure enemy out of a possible ally.

3. STAY IN CHARACTER

After a brief period of association, people such as your subordinates, your staff, and associates learn what to expect from you. If you get out of character when you try to persuade them, they will become suspicious. An arousal of suspicion results in wasted persuasive effort.

For example, a sudden burst of persuasive enthusiasm from an otherwise phlegmatic individual will doom him to failure. Slang from a pedantic professorial type merely for the sake of "talking to the fellows at their own level" is almost certain to boomerang. His audience will lose respect for him and will naturally begin to suspect him of some ill-conceived (for them) plan.

I know that if I were to tell off-color stories in my speeches before management groups, the jokes would get a cool reception. Hopefully, my character is clean humor born in actual situations, not jokes.

So, stay honest. You'll never persuade people with phony techniques or by pretending that you are "one of the boys."

4. AVOID EXAGGERATED PLATITUDES

There are only two situations where persuasive exaggeration can be used to effect. One is politics, which has the peculiar distinction of being a dead-serious game. After the game most participants forget and forgive their opponents. Under these circumstances, exaggeration is part of the fun.

The other situation where persuasive exaggeration is effective is when you know, in advance, that your audience is with you from the time you first open your mouth. When individuals are convinced you are right before you start, then exaggeration will serve to reinforce their resolve and bolster their confidence.

However, if there is any doubt as to how the audience stands, then you must avoid the advertising vocabulary, the exaggeration, and the platitudes. People simply do not respond to gross exaggeration. In addition, exaggeration is an excess that reflects poorly on both your judgment and your taste. If your idea or proposal is truly excellent, it should not be belittled by exaggeration.

5. PLAY DOWN THE FEAR THEME

Fear has some value in persuasion, but it has limited value. Do not depend on it to carry your argument.

One of the best examples of why fear is not wholly effective comes out of World War II. American servicemen overseas were cautioned about the perils of venereal disease. (Remember, "You're damaging government property?") Sickening films threw great fear into the men. The general pattern was that servicemen avoided women for a week or so following these lectures but then they began to pursue the women with more enthusiasm than ever before.

This fear approach didn't work because fear was used excessively; not enough stress was put on the *prevention* of venereal disease. Fear of catching disease had such a highly emotional impact that the men became *frightened* of the disease—so frightened that they forgot how to prevent it.

Stressing the *consequences* of one's act, rather than preventive measures, may result in the avoidance of prevention. A far better approach is to use fear in mild doses, plus heavy concentration upon prevention and caution.

Men forget prevention when they become afraid because of the psychological defense mechanism known as "denial." A man will deny the consequences of his own act, thus do nothing to prevent the consequences.

For example, when you are driving and see a car cracked up along the roadside, you use denial. You may slow down for a few moments, but then you quickly deny that such a thing could happen to you; you resume your former speed. Rarely do your thoughts dwell on ways to prevent accidents: checking your brakes, aligning your steering, cleaning your windshield, and inspecting your tires.

I frequently get annoyed with highway safety programs which use fear excessively when announcing the auto death tolls on national holidays. The way the announcements are made, it sounds as if someone hopes to make the quota of deaths!

When I'm driving, I don't pay any attention to those figures. I deny the possibility that I may become a statistic, because the persuasion, the appeal, is made mostly on fear, not on prevention.

6. AVOID PUSHING FOR IMMEDIATE COMPLIANCE

Pushing for immediate compliance sometimes works in: (1) sex, when you want to take advantage of a present opportunity; (2) selling, when you want a man to put his name on the dotted line; and in (3) charity appeals, when tomorrow may be too late ("Make your pledge *now!*").

But in most other situations, the push for immediate compliance will not have lasting results. It is okay if you are trying to inspire a man for the moment, but if you are trying to persuade a person to change his long-held habits or attitudes, don't demand immediate action. Give him a chance to think it over.

The danger you run in pushing for immediate compliance is the possibility that employees may later think they have been hoodwinked, tricked and conned. This means that all your persuasive effort will have gone for nought.

Do you have to wait indefinitely for compliance? No. While permitting a man to mull over your argument, set a timetable for decision- and opinion-making. If you are asking a subordinate to consider a transfer, give him a few days to ponder the possibilities and discuss them with his wife. Whatever his eventual decision, chances are he'll be happier with it and so will you.

President Johnson knows the value of this technique. As James Reston pointed out in a column for *The New York Times,* Johnson rarely *pushes* for a Congressman's immediate support. He merely exhausts the man. Inviting a Senator to the White House, for example, Johnson will talk to him for hours on a dozen topics before getting to the point.

"Then," Reston observed, "Johnson will argue his case. He will defend it until any opposition from the Senator will seem like treason or worse. Then he will expound on all his troubles from Vietnam and the Congo, to the Caribbean and Mississippi, and finally ask the poor exhausted man on his way to the door, 'Can I count on you?'" The record shows that Johnson's persuasive techniques have proven effective.

When you give someone a short "think it over" period before asking for a commitment, you also give him a chance to vent his emotions. He may need an opportunity to get things off his chest, and he may come to you with some very real, to him, objections to the change you are asking for. Watch him carefully; you may learn something that will give you an advantage. You may be able to find out what is *really* bothering him, which means that now you will direct your future persuasive efforts directly at a specific target. Consequently, your persuasion can be made more effective.

I once met a top executive who frequently negotiates mergers. So doing, he invokes the "do not push for immediate compliance" principle. He always starts with the idea that he will take his time and determine what it is about the merger that appeals or does not appeal to his adversary. Maybe the other fellow wants money. Maybe security. Maybe his wife wants something. At any rate, he never rushes the negotiations until he is positive about the other fellow's goals and is prepared to make an offer along these lines. "If I push too early without knowing the real target," he told me, "it results in an intellectual exercise rather than a deal."

7. GET THE GROUP BEHIND YOU

When others have the same attitudes and philosophies as you, get them to lend you their support.

The deviants, those whom you are trying to persuade, cannot ignore the influence if others rally to your aid. When a person feels isolated from the mainstream of thinking around him, he gets tense and panicky. Tests have shown that a man will often betray his own good judgment in order to conform.

Groups that present a united front exert tremendous pressure on mavericks. When with a group of key employees you approach a loner and say, "Everyone else agrees to our plan, why don't you?", the man will probably change. He'll look for a graceful way of making the change. Perhaps he'll tell himself, "I don't think I understood your reasons the first time," or "I've been thinking it over and I think the plan has value." (You can help him by finding some face-saving way for him to change his mind, such as presenting him with new evidence.)

How do you get the group behind you? Here are some suggestions for use in implementing sweeping changes:

When weighing the possibilities before a decision is made, get wide participation. Solicit suggestions from many people. Encourage democratic participation. Give everyone who might be affected a chance to speak up. A man will support that which he helps to create.

Then, when the decision is reached, post the *group* decision. Immediately, pressure is exerted on those who do not conform. Persuasion of the remaining few will be much easier than if group support was never brought to bear. However, one word of caution: Don't solicit group participation *after* the decision is made. Suggestions should be used, or at least considered, in advance of the decision.

When you must persuade an individual on a matter of interest only to him, you should employ group pressure by enlisting the support of his peers, men whom he respects and admires. Have them line up with you and make sure he finds out about it. There is much truth in the honored expression, "Fifty million Frenchmen can't be wrong." They *may* be wrong, but at least they will all be wrong together.

8. ESTABLISH YOUR EXPERTNESS AND AUTHORITY

Do you argue with a doctor when he persuades you to have an operation? Do you deny your auto mechanic when he persuades you to buy a new fuel pump? In both cases, you are being persuaded by experts, with authoritative credentials. In both cases, their persuasion works.

You can exert the same influence if you strive to establish *your* credentials as an expert. The public believes experts. Witness the success of advertising based on testimony of experts, national heroes, authorities, and prestige and status figures such as athletes and entertainers.

It isn't easy to establish yourself as an expert or authority. It takes time. In business, people come to respect your opinions with more conviction if you *demonstrate* that you have the ability and talent you say you have. Your subordinates must regard you as being worthy of their trust. A title of authority helps, but it is no guarantee.

A word of advice. Never attempt to set yourself up as an authority in too many areas, or you will find yourself losing credibility in areas where you may rightfully be an expert. Many people try to generalize their authority from one subject to another, and most are unsuccessful. I thought that Albert Einstein was a genius when it came to physics, but I disagreed with many things he said on politics.

If you must make decisions and persuade people in areas in which you cannot operate with authority and assurance, admit it. Preface your attempt at persuasion by saying, "I'm not an expert in this area, but I have *talked* with experts. Here's what they advise, and I'm inclined to agree." Then continue. You are very likely to be perceived as a credible and highly regarded source of information, which is almost as good as being an expert!

And, of course, if you *are* rightfully an expert, gently remind your audience of this during your discussion. It will strengthen your argument.

9. TRY TO SATISFY NEEDS

All God's children have needs. If you can find out what is bothering your employees, and try in some way to satisfy their needs, you will find it relatively easy to convince them to do as you wish.

For example, if you know that a supervisor is in need of some ego-building, and if you want to transfer him to another division, you might easily persuade him to make the change if you also agree to give him a fancy title. He'll make the change willingly to satisfy his need for more status.

A problem many managers encounter is, that in trying to satisfy the needs of employees as well as themselves, they are prone to settle for unhappy compromises. Do not look for the compromise. Look outside the boundaries of the problem for a solution that satisfies your need as well as that of your employee.

For instance, if you want the window open and your secretary prefers it closed, a compromise would be to move the desks. A better solution that satisfies both needs is air conditioning.

This concept has been labeled by Mary Parker Follett as an "integrated solution." Its essence lies in the fact that there are no losers. Instead of sacrificing your needs for someone else's, or sacrificing his needs for yours, you develop a solution wholly acceptable to both. The persuader with the integrated solution has a large part of his argument won even before he presents his case. He has done his homework.

Chief Justice Earl Warren recognizes the value of the integrated solution in matters coming before the Supreme Court. In a dedication speech at Fordham University he said, "We are rarely called upon to resolve naked conflicts between freedom on the one hand and tyranny on the other. We are faced instead with conflicting demands of two or more competing interests, each apparently legitimate, which have run afoul of one another, and we must resolve such conflicts in the manner which will best preserve alike our strength, our democracy and our individual liberty."

10. BE SINCERE

The United States was at war. A national effort was under way to persuade people to buy bonds.

Kate Smith, the singer, had decided to do her part in the effort, and for 16 consecutive hours she was on the radio selling bonds. At the end of that period she had succeeded in obtaining pledges totalling $39 million.

Dr. Robert K. Merton and a group of social psychologists set to work to find out how it happened. After long study involving many interviews with individuals who had been persuaded to part with their money, Dr. Merton came up with certain bed-rock findings.

The most important key to Kate Smith's success was her sincerity. Everyone interviewed mentioned this. She had succeeded in carrying out Abraham Lincoln's advice: "If you would win a man to your cause, first convince him that you are his sincere friend." She did this in two ways:

• She showed her feelings. People felt that she expected nothing for herself out of the grueling stint, and that she was actually "living" each story she told of the boys overseas, the anxious parents at home and the girl waiting for her lover to return.

• Her unselfish behavior. The nation was impressed by her willingness to take on such a big job under difficult conditions. She went without sleep for many hours, she took a minimum of time for rest, she could have stopped earlier but she didn't, she insisted on giving of herself. The audience felt that such factors as these were proof of her sincerity.

Kate Smith's audience perceived that she had nothing to gain personally by her appeal. This practically guaranteed her sincerity. Moreover, she was a national figure; over a period of years she had built up a sincere relationship with her public.

This is advisable in the case of business executives, too. The impression you make depends on a whole series of past impacts on the people you're dealing with. You must build a general background of sincerity, rather than try to "pull something off" on the spur of the moment.

The one thing you do not wish to convey when you persuade people is the very fact that you are persuading them. Once a man believes that you are manipulating him, he begins to mistrust you. He begins to wonder "what's in it" for you, what do you have to gain personally?

No one takes notes on every little act you perform, reviewing these notes to judge your sincerity whenever you show up with persuasion on your mind. But a consecutive, consistent series of simple transactions, all performed honestly in the name of sincerity, will eventually total up to a nice sincere image of you. Such an image will always be to your advantage.

11. FACILITATE CHANGE

Make it easy to make the change. You may be on the verge of swaying a man to your side when he suddenly discovers that it is physically impossible (or nearly so) to take the action you desire.

So smooth the way for him. If, for example, you are trying to convince a New York executive to try his hand at managing your branch in Little Rock, Ark., send him down there for a week or so "just to look the situation over." Show him how the branch is ready for rapid growth. Give him the sales figures. Give him some literature on Arkansas to take home to his wife. Have a new house all picked out and ready for his inspection. Offer to move his household effects at company expense.

One of the reasons Kate Smith's bond appeal was so effective was that she continuously reminded her audience that it was "easy" to pick up the telephone and pledge a bond, at the very moments when her appeals were most persuasive.

12. PROVIDE RECOGNITION

Bulletin boards that display awards, company newspapers and magazines that carry photographs and stories about individuals, awards and presentations that recognize service, are all part of the persuasion picture. Offer a man a concrete reward, show him that you recognize he may be making a sacrifice, and you are likely to convince him he was right in agreeing to your suggestions.

This *always* works when you are trying to persuade people to part with their money. It is amazing how many people respond to such symbols as plaques or certificates, or even framed letters. I have visited offices of many executives who frame their certificates and place them in honored positions for all to see. One vice-president told me, "Our bishop does it beautifully. He hands out the plaques for last year's contributions and then before the ceremony ends he tells us what he expects for next year, and all of us begin again!"

Another form of recognition is giving others verbal credit for changing their habits and attitudes as you desired. If, for example, a troublemaker among your employees has a negative attitude toward management, and you have been successfully persuading him over a period of months that management is operating in his best interests, play up the change in his attitude. Tell him that you notice a subtle change in his attitude, and that it shows in his behavior, and that you like what you see. Once his position aligns with what you wish, give him full credit for making the change and offer him recognition in the form of additional salary, time off, or even a promotion.

13. BE ENTHUSIASTIC

A moderate amount of flag-waving is helpful. At least convey the impression that your project or idea is appealing.

You must believe in something, and demonstrate that belief through enthusiasm, before you can be successful at persuasion. Your own enthusiasm is the best emotional lubricant for others. When they, too, become enthusiastic, they'll find it easy to agree.

Never convey the idea, when persuading someone, that you are merely going through the motions to satisfy a duty, or that you are just passing along instructions from someone higher up, or that you are merely amusing yourself. Try to be genuine, and show a moderate amount of genuine enthusiasm.

14. PLAY UP PARTICIPATION

Most individuals enjoy the pleasures of participation in a broadly defined project. This is well known to industrial psychologists; they frequently advise a man who must persuade another to use the "team argument." This argument takes many forms, but always pushes the theme, "You can help us. This is a team effort. You can make a strong contribution if you will join our cause. We need you."

In the context of company environments, Dr. Harry Levinson of the Menninger Clinic refers to the phenomenon of reciprocation. Reciprocation is the process of fulfilling one's expectations and gratifying one's needs in an organization. Psychologically, Levinson points out, "Man takes the company to himself." Reciprocation provides a source of self-esteem, support, and reward.

However, when you are trying to convince a man to do something your way, it is important to enlist the action, not merely the *agreement* of the individual to act. Get him started. At the beginning, you may have to spoon-feed the assignments and escort him at every turn. That's acceptable, so long as you begin a gradual withdrawal before he learns to depend on you.

Thus, in persuading the New Yorker to transfer to Arkansas, agree to work hand-in-hand with him until he is completely familiar with the task. Then say, "Once you're familiar with the set-up, I'll withdraw and expect you to pull your share of the load. You'll be a key player on this team if you can operate without my constant supervision."

15. MAKE IT PUBLIC

Once a man tentatively agrees to your plan, ask him to put it on record. For example, you might suggest that the executive announce his move to Arkansas by putting it in the paper; have him check with the personnel department about moving expenses; ask him to recommend someone to take his place.

When you get him to go on record like this, it will insure his continued agreement. Dr. Carl Hovland explains that once a man has taken a stand on an issue and everyone knows it, it becomes embarrassing and emotionally inconvenient for him to change back to his former view. He will persist in the stand he took with you.

This, as some men realize, is a key element in female psychology. When a girl persuades her boy friend to agree to become engaged, it becomes very difficult for the young man to back out of marriage. That's because the engagement is tantamount to a public declaration. The newspapers carry the news, the relatives are informed, arrangements are made for the wedding.

All young ladies who are serious about marriage push for an engagement for this reason.

On the other hand, if the young man were to simply say, "OK. Let's get engaged but we'll keep it private," he has a chance to stall the wedding ceremony forever. No public commitments are made.

In the industrial situation, when a man has agreed with you, make sure he declares himself publicly. If he doesn't, he will be less resistant to counter-influences and less likely to stick with you when the time comes to act.

There are various ways to have him make an agreement public. Writing is one form; ask him to get out a memo to everyone involved. If a major project is involved, get the news out through your public relations department (and make sure credit is given where it will do the most good). Talking up the project at lunch and at meetings is also a convenient way to make a public declaration.

And, the *faster* you make it public, the greater your chances of success.

A case of persuasion in action

Recently, I was approached by the president and board chairman of an international metals company about a problem in persuasion. This chapter concludes with a discussion of the problem—and its solution—because it illustrates effective persuasive techniques, using many of the principles I just presented. At the request of the individuals involved in this incident, I have preserved their anonymity.

The problem: A key executive in this large international enterprise had submitted his resignation to the president and board of directors. "I need this man," the board chairman told me. "He runs my operation in Europe and I can't replace him. I must persuade him to stay. But I am not very effective at persuasion. I almost always lose. The use of fear and threat have never worked for me. Once a man hands me his resignation he almost always has made it public, and this executive is no exception. He's already told his wife and friends. His staff probably knows, too. When I talk to him, I know he is going to say that he is a man of integrity, that he is committed to resign, and that he can't continue to work without a serious loss of face. In addition, I

cannot offer him more money because his friends and associates
will construe this as a bribe. He may not even want to talk to
me for fear that he will be persuaded to stay, losing face.

"What can I do?"

Here is the substance of the advice I gave:

Limited use of fear. Don't threaten him. If, for instance, he
says that he is going into business for himself, or that he is going
to work for a competitor, don't threaten to crush him and make
him sorry that he left. Instead, concentrate on reality. Tell him
that he is taking a risk, that there are vast unknowns when he
goes into business for himself, but that he has some security with
you. He already knows these things; you're just reminding him.

Don't push for immediate compliance. Tell him you would
prefer not to accept the resignation, that you want him to stay.
But don't push for agreement at your first discussion. Take him
out to dinner, give him a few weeks at a resort with his wife at
company expense, tell him to think it over. Then tell him if he
still wants to resign after having a chance to think it over in a
relaxed environment away from the pressures of business, his
resignation will be accepted without another word.

Use prestige and authority supports. Remind him that, in your
position as head of the company, you have access to every fact
and figure that relates to the operating position of the company.
Then say that in reviewing these data, you can only conclude
that the company has a great future. Let him in on some of your
plans for expansion. Tell him what business you anticipate for
the next year.

Be sincere. Remind him that in the past you have encouraged
executives to resign when opportunities did not exist, and that
you would do the same now if this were the case. But, since you
want him to stay, tell him so and be truthful and sincere about
it. In other words, if he is permitted to feel that you are manipulating him only because you need him now, and that he will be
dumped as soon as he can be replaced, then nothing you say
will work. Discuss the pros and cons of his leaving. And, of
course, weigh in your own mind the resignation. If it is better
for him to leave, don't try to hold him; if you do, he will only
become bitter and this will result in hostility later.

Use peer pressure to facilitate matters. Ask some of the other important executives in the company, including some of this man's close associates, to encourage him to stay. Allow them to help you build a bridge back to the company so he can walk away from the resignation and back to the organization with dignity. Chat with some of his peers in the organization. Many of them will *want* the man to stay. Suggest that they call him and talk about his future.

Be sensitive to his needs. Offer him something he wants. This man apparently is anxious for status. Make him a director of the company. If he likes to travel, give him an opportunity to scout out new business opportunities in places he's never visited.

When I last spoke with the president, he reported that he and the board chairman had acted on most of these suggestions. Shortly thereafter, the executive decided to "take another look," at the company before making a final decision. In addition, the chairman and president both learned a valuable lesson in avoiding future problems of a similar nature.

Be honest; don't manipulate

The tools of effective persuasion are now in your hands. These principles are based on years of research by psychologists. However, you should use them only after an honest consideration of needs—yours, the individual's, and the company's. Remember, a manipulator of people (a man who uses rather than motivates subordinates) is doomed to eventual failure.

To paraphrase the words of Norbert Wiener, the founder of cybernetics, the goals of persuasion are "the human use of human beings." The principles should never be used to gain illegitimate power over others, to enhance your own status, or to meet your own selfish ends without regard to the goals and needs of others.

10.

The Art of
Constructive
Criticism

A bank president I know once gave a speech titled, "Kill the Umpire." He chose this title because he was the umpire in his company's game; he was calling the balls and strikes on his executives.

The functions of the umpire and the corporate manager are very much alike in many respects. *Someone* has to call them as he sees them. John Lear, science editor of the *Saturday Review,* draws the analogy for managers like this:

> How long would *you* last if you had to do *your* job in an open arena, before thousands of excited, shouting people? Especially if you were assailed with words like "thief," punctuated occasionally with flying pop bottles?
>
> However, if you did manage to hold out, the world would know that a manager's job is even more exacting than an umpire's. For you too have got to call them, while playing as a member of the home team!

Managers have the advantage over umpires of being able to coach, criticize, and praise the players when it seems appropriate. But the manager's job is tougher than the umpire's in yet another respect: The umpire calls his decisions as he makes them, the plainer the better for the sake of the crowd; the manager must call what he sees at different times and in different ways, depending on his judgment of the effect on his men.

This chapter will take you through the supermarket of criticism. It will teach you how to be fair—how to be objective. It will point out what aspects of criticism to buy, what to pass up, and what will be accepted by the members of your staff. In short, it may even help your people say, with Winston Churchill:

"I do not resent criticism even when for the sake of emphasis it parts for the time with reality."

Why others ask for criticism

By all psychological standards, criticism should be accepted as routine. The manager must do it, and every employee wants to know where he stands. Most good workers, in fact, will say that they know they need improvement. But behind the open invitation to criticize lie many hidden resistances.

Ted Williams, one of baseball's greatest hitters, said, "When somebody says nice things about me, it goes in one ear and out the other. But I remember the criticism longer. I hate criticism—and the sportswriters who write the way they feel instead of what they've actually seen."

When someone asks you to evaluate his performance, consider for a moment:

* Does he really want reassurance and approval or confirmation of what he is to do?
* Does he really want an honest opinion?
* Does he suspect you're about to evaluate him anyway and try to take some of the edge off by asking for it before he receives it?
* Can he accept an admonition to change? Can he accept the possibility of failure which may develop?

All of these reasons may lie behind a request for an evaluation. You may not be able to determine which one applies. However, an understanding that there may be more behind the request than meets the ear, will give you some pause before answering.

Always state criticism in clear and absolute terms

Executives are generally poorly equipped to play the role of critics. They are usually energetic, driving, have a tendency to see things that escape others, have little tolerance for sloppy work. All these reasons cause them to jump in and make changes.

Some executives believe, deep down, that G. B. Shaw was right when he said that, "In this world, if you do not say anything in an irritating way, you may just as well not say it at all, since nobody will trouble themselves about anything that does not trouble them. The attention given to criticism is in direct proportion to its indigestibility."

The successful executive cannot deny himself the outlet of distasteful criticism. He cannot thwart it; *he must control it*—hold it in proper bounds. He cannot pounce on a man when something goes wrong, but must ask for reasons, seek extenuating circumstances, remind himself of personal idiosyncracies and the problems he knows this particular individual is harassed by. Above all, he must listen respectfully to the defenses and complaints that are offered.

Some executives try to avoid the problem by going to the opposite extreme and priding themselves on *never* criticizing. Some criticize but try to make it painless. These are the men who damn with faint praise and praise with superlatives.

These men fool no one but themselves. Their words are accepted in the same perspective as advertisements for motion pictures. "Colossal" means "poor," "stupendous" means "fair," "world-shaking" means "mediocre." "Swell picture" doesn't even draw an audience.

The man who thinks he never criticizes is constantly in danger of being considered critical. What he intends as a friendly "hello" may, for momentary lack of exaggerated enthusiasm, be interpreted as a reprimand.

Moral: Don't leave it to your men to read your real reactions. They may read you wrong.

This point was punctuated in a case cited by *New Yorker* Magazine: A committee of teachers in a junior high school on Long Island was appointed by the principal to find ways of saying things more tactfully on report cards. The committee made these recommendations:

Hard	*Softer*
Too free with fists	Resorts to physical means of winning his point or attracting attention.
Could stand more baths; dirty; has bad odor	Needs guidance in development of good habits of hygiene.
Lies	Shows difficulty in distinguishing between imaginary and factual material.
Cheats	Needs help in learning to adhere to rules and standards of fair play.
Steals	Needs help in learning to respect the property rights of others.
Insolent	Needs guidance in learning to express himself respectfully.
Lazy	Needs ample supervision in order to work well.
Selfish	Needs help in learning to enjoy sharing with others.
Noisy	Needs to develop quieter habits of communication.
Is a bully	Has qualities of leadership but needs help in learning to use them democratically.

Lesson for managers: Don't mince words with your men. State your criticism clearly and in absolute terms. That way there will be no doubt exactly where you stand.

Many managers mistakenly believe that criticism is discouraging, that it destroys morale and makes enemies out of subordinates.

That's folly. I've already stated that many employees *need* criticism. Beyond that, I want to assure you that as long as criticism (1) gives the worker all the information he needs to improve his performance, and (2) is objective and free of personal feelings, then you have nothing to worry about. Under such conditions, no reasonable employee can consider criticism an attack. When an employee is unreasonable, then nothing you say will help.

Fourteen guides for effective criticism

Don't look for hard and fast rules in criticism. There are none. Two people and two situations are never completely similar.

Yet rules are valuable because, as George Orwell points out, "One needs rules that one can rely on when instinct fails."

Here, then, are some guidelines to help you criticize without alienation, to be forthright without being caustic, to be incisive without being abusive:

1. DON'T WASTE YOUR TIME

Your time as a manager is valuable; don't waste it criticizing an employee unless you feel that he is capable of making some improvement. As we say in psychotherapy, the employee who is deficient must have some "capacity for movement" to be worth your effort.

Bernard Baruch and Herbert Bayard Swope once had a tremendous disagreement. Swope wrote Baruch, saying:

"We have fought much and laughed often, but almost always on the same side. Now we find ourselves in disagreement. I want you to know that no matter what happens, I have great admiration for your strengths and compassion for your deficiencies."

As a manager, if you can have admiration for a man's strengths and compassion for his deficiencies, you can tell him almost anything and expect him to acknowledge it. But if you *don't* have admiration for his strengths, don't waste time trying to improve the deficiencies.

2. PICK THE TIME CAREFULLY

If you are criticizing an employee for a single undesirable action, then by all means make your negative comments immediately upon his completion of the act. Correct him immediately.

But if you are criticizing constructively in terms of your employee's long-range self, as you would during a performance review, then try to pick your time so that it will support your cause.

Most managers think the best time to criticize is at the end of the week. They believe that Friday afternoon is a good time for a heart-to-heart talk.

Actually, this may be the worst time. The manager rushes through his lecture and the subordinate goes home for a miserable weekend. He spends all Saturday and Sunday licking his wounds; by Monday morning he is ready for combat.

The same reaction occurs when you make a negative comment in the evening or at quitting time. As Frank Boyden, head of the well-known Deerfield Academy, points out, "Never reprimand in the evening; darkness and troubled minds are a poor combination."

Why not make your negative evaluation in the morning, at the beginning of the week? This way, a gesture or a wave of your hand will indicate to the individual that the past is over with, and that an improving relationship can be maintained.

Time a reprimand so that you have another chance to talk to the individual before the day is over. The chat after the correction need be nothing more than a few casual words showing that your sincere feelings toward the person have not diminished, that you're sure the fault will be corrected, or that the long range security of the individual on the job has not been threatened.

It isn't necessary to express these ideas in exactly these sentences. It's the attitude, the *feeling* tone, that registers.

3. BE INVOLVED

Criticize your man in an environment where he knows you are paying direct attention to him. If possible, go to *his* work station rather than have him come to yours. If you are forced to talk to him in your own office, however:

- don't dance around your desk,
- don't stare thoughtfully out the window,
- don't rummage through your drawers, and
- have your secretary cut off all telephone calls and all visitors.

The object is to make your man realize that at this moment, he is the most important thing on your mind. In a sense, this is flattery, but it helps if he thinks he means something to you.

4. KNOW THE TARGET

Just what kind of person is the man you're going to criticize? Is he receptive? Defensive? Is he looking for ways to improve?

Let's go back to the baseball park. The late John McGraw, colorful manager of the old New York Giants, was a rough, tough character. Back in 1916 he wanted Buck Herzog as his second baseman. "I don't like you and you don't like me," he told Herzog. "But I need you on my ball club."

"There's no need for us to be friends," Herzog said. "You're the greatest manager in baseball. Although I don't like you, I'll give you my best." And he did.

Over on the New York Yankee bench, in the same era, Manager Miller Huggins tried for years to get along with home run king Babe Ruth. The Babe responded with utter contempt to any and all kinds of criticism from Huggins. The manager could have called for a showdown, but put it off. Finally, one day Ruth arrived at the park late for a game:

"Don't bother to get into uniform today," Huggins blazed. "You're indefinitely suspended and fined $5,000."

Only after that did the big slugger heed his manager's words—and only then, incidentally, did Huggins win the respect of the rest of his team.

But with your employees, particularly women, gentle, reassuring suggestions work best. If you're not certain, play it safe. Use the gentle approach. Reassurance that they can do better, with faith in their ability to change, can make the harshest sounding criticism palatable.

5. TAKE ONE POINT AT A TIME

The tendency with many managers, once they get started in a critical interview, is to give their subordinates a critical broadside; they over-criticize.

I've seen it often. An executive starts to criticize a staff man. The subordinate nods, agrees, seems to understand, and is entirely cooperative. Suddenly the executive lets loose with all his complaints. He really unloads the pent-up criticism of weeks, months. "Why not?", the manager rationalizes to himself. "I've got him on the run; he seems to accept criticism!"

Too much criticism is extremely destructive. Moreover, the subordinate may lose perspective; he may not know which problems you are most concerned about and which are less important. He surely won't know where to begin correcting his behavior or attitudes.

But if you concentrate on only one point in your criticism, he knows what you want him to do. Next month, when he's solved that problem, then you can talk to him about something else that's bothering you.

6. KEEP IT PRIVATE

Public criticism can be, and frequently is, disastrous. It burns itself into the mind and may never be erased.

Even public figures, who are accustomed to being criticized in public, are bothered by lack of privacy when it comes to negative commentary.

The famous actress Ethel Barrymore, in her "Memoirs," tells of a critical comment that she never forgot. She had played a character named Madame Trentoni, and this is what one newspaper's theater columnist wrote: "If the young lady who played Madame Trentoni had possessed beauty, charm or talent this play might have been a success."

To Miss Barrymore, after more than 50 years, those words were still the "only criticism I have ever been able to remember word for word."

Would the outraged actress have felt less stung if the critic had addressed her privately? Perhaps in her dressing room? Would the pain have been eased still further if the criticism had been delayed to a relaxed moment?

No one develops a skin thick enough to ward off criticism. Bob Hope once told me, "I was always hurt by being taken over the coals in print for everyone to see. I still am. But I've tried to handle it by putting up two clippings in my dressing room. One reads, 'Hope is the Greatest Living Comedian' and the other 'Hope is the Biggest Skunk in the World.'"

When it comes to criticism, greatness responds no differently from ordinary human beings.

So you can safely add Ethel Barrymore and Bob Hope to your list of reasons for being thoughtful of the circumstances when you criticize on the job.

7. CRITICIZE CONSTRUCTIVELY

Criticism, to be effective, must be specific. It must equip the worker with all the information he needs for a good performance.

Psychologists call this "knowledge of results." One study found that providing specific information helped make apprentices better than experienced journeymen who had been on the job for years. The experimenter determined the number of errors made by journeymen in reading micrometers. Then, he took a group of apprentices and gave them a seven-hour training program in which they measured a series of blocks. After each measurement, he told them where they were off and specifically how they could improve. *There were no general statements, but rather, specific suggestions of what could be done and why.*

In criticizing your subordinate, don't say "You haven't got the right attitude" or "You should be more careful." Tell him the details left undone, the deadlines missed, or the extra costs incurred because of his errors.

Relate your criticism to the job. Except for the rarest of exceptions (when his off-the-job activities would have definite adverse effect on the company), you have the right to criticize him only in the areas where he fails to do his best and thereby lets you and the company down.

8. NEVER SAY "ALWAYS"

"Always" is a form of exaggeration; it distorts the degree of a man's fault. Sometimes "always" will help him to erect a defense against what is only a minor point.

I'll give you an example. I smoke a pipe and cigars. My wife says I'm *always* throwing ashes on the floor of the living room. Well, I'm not *always* doing it. I only do it when I can't find an ashtray.

You see, I'm wrong. I should *never* throw ashes on the floor.

But I'm defensive about it because my wife accuses me of *always* doing it.

So, avoid the use of the word "always." Strike it from your managerial vocabulary.

9. FACE FACTS SQUARELY

The "sandwich technique" of praise-and-criticism has been widely and, I think, mistakenly advocated. To sandwich a man, you start with a compliment to create a glow. Then you throw in some comments on weaknesses. Finally, you close with more compliments. This works out in a number of ways, none of them good.

First, there is the danger that the employee won't even hear the criticism. He may remember only his virtues, which (to add to his confusion) are usually stated more firmly and in greater detail than his failings. Second, the criticism *may* come through; even if it does, it may hurt worse for cutting through a compliment. Besides, the employee may recognize it as a technique and resent it as insincere.

The assumption must be that any criticism you give your subordinate is for his own good. Therefore, why stall? The discussion might follow this sequence instead: first his weaknesses, second his strengths, third the future.

Say the negative things first because, when you say the positive things later, you will help to begin the healing process.

10. DON'T MAKE A JOKE OF IT

The story is told that Ely Culbertson once watched a woman massacre a hand at bridge. When it was over, she asked, "Mr. Culbertson, how would you have played that hand?" He replied, "Under an assumed name."

There's always a temptation to use the light touch in criticism, but like Culbertson's light touch, it will probably seem pretty heavy handed to the victim. Few people have the gift of conveying criticism through kindly humor.

Your well-meant joke may sound very sarcastic to your subordinate. It may make him feel small. Even if he accepts it with outward good humor, he may still feel that you're taking him and his problem too lightly.

Play it straight and leave the humor to the comics.

11. ATTACK THE ACT

Any statement of criticism must be objective and free of any personal feeling on your part which the worker could possibly interpret as an attack. The criticism must always be directed to what can be done, rather than to the person.

The ideal attitude toward criticism was expressed by a child during an experiment. Each pupil in this class was asked to write down the names of classmates he liked, and those he didn't. One child wrote no names in either category, explaining, "I like all of my classmates, but I don't always like everything they do."

This remarkable pupil may not have fully realized the pitfalls he was avoiding by criticizing what people *do*, rather than criticizing the people themselves. Many adults are equally oblivious of the paralyzing consequences of doing things the other way around. Criticism that can be interpreted as personal attack not only fails to clear up mistakes but actually worsens performance. Persons criticized under such circumstances rarely absorb what you tell them. Everyone likes to keep a high opinion of himself, as I indicated earlier. By attacking a man's self-image you only succeed in producing hostility and damaged feelings. So, tell him what's wrong with his work—not, what's wrong with himself.

12. RECOGNIZE YOUR OWN POWER

Criticism carries a message about the critic. Listen:

"That's no way to handle that job, Jones. If you had asked me, I would have shown you how to avoid all that trouble." This supervisor may really be afraid that Jones does not respect his greater experience.

It is important for you to recognize your own needs. They can greatly influence your use of power over subordinates. You may not think of yourself as a person of real influence. But to your subordinates you may be the most influential person in the company—particularly at those moments that call for criticism.

In his book *The Forgotten Language,* Erich Fromm, the famous psychoanalyst, tells of a dream that a patient described to a psychoanalyst. The patient was a lawyer, 28 years old, and the dream was as follows·

"I saw myself riding on a white charger, reviewing a large number of soldiers. They all cheered me wildly."

What had happened the day before to set off the dream that night?

The lawyer had gathered material for a legal brief and had submitted it to the senior partner of his law firm. The senior partner, discovering an error in the legal logic, fixed the young man with a critical eye and remarked, "I'm really surprised—I had thought you would do better than that."

Where did the white horse and the cheering soldiers come from?

Well, when the young lawyer was a boy, he was weak and scrawny. Bigger boys laughed at him. Then he read about Napoleon, a little guy that big guys didn't laugh at. So he dreamed about being Napoleon. And even after many years had passed, and he was no longer weak or scrawny or laughed at, that one criticism from his boss made the young lawyer wonder whether he would lose his chance to be a partner in the law firm.

Unconsciously, he fought off the threat to his future by getting on Napoleon's horse and riding in triumphal review through the troops of his dreams.

How could the senior partner of the law firm know all that? Obviously, he couldn't. But if he had worded his criticism to sound less like a judge's sentence, Napoleon's horse would have enjoyed a well-earned rest that night.

13. CRITICIZE WITHOUT COMPARISON

It is a basic psychological principle that people can compete most effectively and with greater productivity if they compete against themselves.

Criticism will be accepted with less resistance if your subordinate is shown how he can do better, rather than by comparing his past performance with others. Most of us want acceptance within the limits of our own abilities. "Show me how I can do better, not by comparisons with someone else, but rather by pointing up what there is within that I can change," is the unspoken cry.

In addition, unfavorable comparisons produce hostility within your own work group. In one company, a skilled workman explained to an interviewer why he resented his supervisor: "In our shop there's one operator who can never do anything wrong. That's the way Joe, our supervisor, looks at it. He always holds that man up to us as a model."

The men resented this comparison. They felt that they were *all* skilled operators, and that, while they made mistakes, no man was so inferior to the others that he deserved to be singled out and criticized.

On the other hand, you might try *favorable* comparison, such as "You certainly learn faster than anyone else here," or "If you can lick the controls on that power press, you'll be the most valuable man in the shop."

One road leads to hostility towards you and loss of faith in the employee's ability; the other road produces a sense of confidence in his ability to perform the task at hand.

14. DON'T EXPECT POPULARITY AS AN UMPIRE

Even if you had all the wisdom in the world, criticism is bound to strike a sour note occasionally. But it isn't really your job to make friends. Your job is to be respected, and so to get the work done. After all, as Sigmund Freud pointed out, work is man's strongest tie to the real world in which he lives.

The umpires of big league baseball rarely had rhubarbs to contend with when they called double-plays executed by Tinkers and Evers and Chance. These three players worked so smoothly together that double-plays were practically automatic with them. But Tinkers, Evers, and Chance hated each other. That understanding supervision was all that held them together, did not even occur to the screaming throngs who packed the bleachers.

Why managers can't avoid criticism

Still don't feel right when it comes time to criticize your employees? Perhaps this concluding thought will give you confidence:

You have no right to duck. You are accountable for the performance of the people in your department, and you must be ready both to give and receive criticism. In fact, you *owe* it to your subordinates to criticize them and show them how to improve.

Remember, an indictment that nestles in the back of your head deprives an individual of his democratic right of self-defense. As Marshall Field once said, "Those who come to flatter, please me. Those who complain, teach me how I may please others so that more will come. Only those hurt me who are displeased but do not complain. They refuse me permission to correct my errors and thus improve my service."

11.

How to Manage
Creative People

Every executive realizes that in the world of business, creativity is a rare and prized characteristic. The person who consistently comes up with an imaginative solution to a persistent, nagging, chronic problem—whether he is the custodian or the controller—will always win the respect of his fellow men.

Proper *management* of creativity is one of the really difficult challenges facing business and industry today, for creativity is of no value to a company unless it is discovered and exploited to its fullest potential. Moreover, this challenge of managing creativity extends through the entire functional spectrum of management, from selection of the creative individual, to criticism and admonition.

Despite the great need for information on managing creativity, it has only been within the past 15 years or so that creative people have been given any significant attention by psychologists. Until recently, most applied and industrial psychologists have been too busy delving into other fields to give creativity the attention it deserves. As a result, for example, we know relatively little about creative employees (including creative executives)—what motivates them, what depresses them, how they function. Similarly, little is known about how to get non-creative personnel to work in a more creative manner.

This is not to say that there is total ignorance on the subject. I am merely stating that there is less knowledge, experimentation, and research about creative people to draw upon, than there is in other fields of human behavior. In this chapter, I will set forth some of what *is* known about the management and utilization of creativity, and I will synthesize and present it in a manner which will be useful to the operating executive.

For ease of presentation and understanding, I have divided this chapter into two sections:

1. How to make yourself a more creative manager.
2. How to stimulate your creative employees to greater productivity.

Make yourself more creative

There are those who say that creativity is a miracle of nature, that it "just happens." In fact, Tchaikovsky once compared creative compositions to an act of nature:

"If the soil is ready," he said, "the germ of a future composition takes root with extraordinary force and rapidity, shoots up through the earth, puts forth branches, leaves and finally blossoms. I cannot describe the creative process in any other way than by this simile."

But creativity, in its simplest and most usual form, is really only a variation of problem-solving. It is little more than an exercise in attacking a mental challenge.

If you were to take apart the creative process and analyze its components, you'll find that there are always four stages in the development of creative thought:

1. PREPARATION. This is the stage in which you become acquainted with the problem, or the mental challenge. It involves learning what must be accomplished. It may consist of a formal approach, involving lengthy investigation and many discussions. Or, it may be merely a general mental awareness, such as the knowledge of a particular professional specialty or project or organization. In a sense, a manager's background and experience

are preparation for creative problem-solving. Remember what Tchaikovsky said? "If the soil is ready. . ." He knew the value of preparation.

2. INCUBATION. This is the stage when the mind appears to be inactive but, in reality, is turning over all the possibilities in the unconscious. Usually, you are not even aware of what is going on inside your mind because you may be engaged in other activities at the time. Patience is a virtue in this stage.

3. ILLUMINATION. This is the stage when the mind comes up with a good idea. It may be the basic solution to your problem, or perhaps it is the insight you need to open up a whole new field of thought. Sometimes this illumination comes suddenly; things seem to fall into place. You may jump up in the middle of the night with the idea you've waited weeks to find.

4. VERIFICATION. The last stage in the process, verification, occurs when you refine the idea and determine if it works. This is also the stage of judgment and decision-making.

I have observed that executives are, generally speaking, more creative in some of these stages than others. I have seen, for example, many executives who simply cannot come up with a new idea, but who are great when it comes to separating the good ones from the bad. Some managers are effective sifters of solutions to problems; they are critics; they can do wonderful things when it comes to promoting and merchandising ideas. But if they were asked to come up with some new ideas themselves, they'd be hard put to comply.

The point I want to make is that there are many ways to be creative. Generating ideas is only one way. You don't have to come up with the ideas in order to be a creative manager, and you don't have to be able to merchandise them in order to be creative. Creativity takes many forms, and rarely will all characteristics be found in the same person.

The blocks to creativity

What are the blocks, the hurdles, to creativity?

There are some very definite reasons why people aren't more creative. They fall into two broad but well-defined categories: psychological reasons and perceptual reasons.

PSYCHOLOGICAL BLOCKS

1. *It takes time to develop a new idea.* It is much more expedient to go along with what is presently being done, than to develop a totally new approach. In business and industry, most executives simply do not have the time to study problems and to permit their minds the luxury of wandering through the four steps we just discussed.

2. *It takes a thick skin.* Many people who develop new ideas are regarded as odd-balls. A creative manager has to expose himself to harsh critical judgment by his peers and superiors—just for the sake of being different and bucking the tide of conformity. Sometimes evaluation of creativity takes the form of ridicule, satire and personal degradation. It takes a thick skin to propose new ideas, and then to expose both the ideas and yourself to the rejection treatment.

3. *It takes dedication and commitment.* Eventually, every creative person encounters some hostility. No one has ever come up with a new, worthwhile idea without encountering some hostility from people who believed 100 per cent in the old idea, and who refused to accept the new. We all know people who hold their own ideas as sacred. Thus, in order to sell your new idea and see that it wins acceptance, you have to be totally committed to it. If you aren't, how can you convince others of its merit?

4. *Your status may be threatened when you come up with a new idea.* Suppose, for example, that you go to great extremes to develop, propose, or sell a new approach to a nagging problem. Everyone stakes his all on you. Then, your approach is a total failure. It flops. How does this affect your status? Certainly it has come down a notch or two.

PERCEPTUAL BLOCKS

Your mental frame of reference blocks you from looking at an old problem from a new angle.

For example, this simple test will show you how your frame of reference restricts your ability to solve problems:

Sample problem. Suppose you had two water containers and

an unlimited supply of water. One container can hold 29 quarts, the other 3 quarts. How would you measure out 20 quarts?

Answer. Fill the 29-quart container, then remove 3 quarts three times with the 3-quart container. Or: 29-3-3-3 = 20

Now here are three similar problems, each involving three containers.

1. You have the following containers:

31	61	4	
qts.	qts.	qts.	- get 22 qts.

Your solution:

2. You have the following containers:

23	51	4	
qts.	qts.	qts.	- get 20 qts.

Your solution:

3. You have the following containers:

5	15	20	
qts.	qts.	qts.	- get 10 qts.

Your solution:

Psychologists use this experiment to demonstrate how your frame of reference can cause "mental rigidity." The first two problems condition you with a series of subtractions.

1. 61 - 31 - 4 - 4 = 22 qts.
2. 51 - 23 - 4 - 4 = 20 qts.

Because that pattern has been set in your thinking, you follow the same frame of reference and go through unnecesary steps to get the answer to No. 3. The short, direct route, of course, should be to use the five-quart container twice.

In business, you can't afford to let the wrong frame of reference take you the long way 'round. Your personal success depends on your ability to break the usual frame of reference and find the better, shorter, and cheaper way.

Another problem psychologists use to show how a frame of reference inhibits creative thought, is the "nine-dot" problem. Connect these nine dots with four single lines, without lifting your pencil from the paper:

```
•   •   •

•   •   •

•   •   •
```

The answer appears at the top of page 186.

As you can see, the problem can only be solved by going *outside* the frame of reference.

How you can jump the hurdles

So now that I have demonstrated the hurdles that prevent you from being more creative, I will proceed to explain how to break the blocks.

The *psychological* hurdles present barriers that only you can climb. As I explained, you need time, a thick skin, dedication, and a willingness to accept defeat, to help you with the psychology of creativity. These are things which I cannot give you; you must acquire them for yourself.

What I will present here are ways to help you change your *frame of reference*. In psychological terminology this is known as "breaking a set," or shattering a frame of reference. Set-breaking is the most important prerequisite to creative thinking. Here are seven ways to satisfy that requirement.

1. TURN IT UPSIDE DOWN

To get a new perspective on a landscape, a Japanese artist starts by looking at it upside down. He turns around, bends down, puts his head between his knees and observes the scene. Photographers, when composing portraits, look at their subjects upside down through the lens. This helps to establish new patterns of lines.

If you want to turn your problem upside down, ask questions like these:

What if this were reversed? Suppose cause and effect were reversed? If it's horizontal, suppose it were vertical? If vertical, suppose it were horizontal. If it's long, suppose it were short? If short, long? If high, low? If low, high? If inside, outside? If outside, inside? If on top, suppose it were on the bottom?

Henry Ford used this technique successfully to create the assembly line. All industrialists were looking for ways to bring employees to the materials and production area. Ford reversed his thinking, and brought the production area and materials to the employees. The idea of the assembly line emerged and later became the basis of mass production.

2. CHALLENGE YOUR ASSUMPTIONS

Say it isn't so. Columbus, Hudson, Magellan and other explorers challenged what everyone was taking for granted and opened up a whole new world. Pasteur challenged assumptions in medicine, Einstein in physics, Edison in several fields. In challenging assumptions that clouded and restricted others, these men found new paths to better ideas.

Ask questions like these to challenge your own assumptions:

Does it have to be this way? Could it be that way? Does it have to be done here? Why not there? We've always taken this approach; why not the other approach?

A New Jersey food processor had a problem disposing of empty concentrate cans. Four men driving two trucks were required to cart the cans to a dumping area—an expensive, unproductive operation. While everyone tried to answer the question, "How can we dispose of cans quickly and more cheaply?", one creative manager asked, "Why throw them away at all?" He broke the frame of reference by challenging the assumption of disposal. Today, the firm *sells* its empty concentrate cans as scrap.

3. TEAR IT APART

Take the item (or old technique) apart, piece by piece, attribute by attribute. Just list the elements; then, go over them one by one, looking for some new relationships among them.

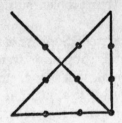

(Answer to problem on page 184).

Ask yourself questions like these:

What are the different parts of the problem? Is one of them the key to another part? Do I have to change any parts? Suppose I changed the timing, the size, the form, the color?

Professor Robert Crawford at the University of Nebraska explains this technique admirably. Here's how he would tear apart a picture frame:

The shape is rectangular; but could it be round, elliptical, continuous like a mural, three-dimensional like a shadow box? The material is wood; but could it also be plaster, aluminum, plastic, glass, or even no material at all (no frame)? The covering is glass; but couldn't it be lucite, or a shade, or nothing? The support is a wire hanger; but could it also be a brace, or a shelf, or a free-standing tripod?

4. CHANGE THE ORDER

Once you know the parts of your problem, you can change your frame of reference merely by re-arranging them. The child who uses a toy kaleidoscope rearranges the parts every time he turns the tube. And every time the parts are rearrangd, the child sees a new picture, a new alignment. He has literally changed his frame of reference.

Try these questions to change the order and rearrange the parts of your problem:

Suppose I juggle the parts? Can I separate the elements that are now together? Can I bring together those elements that are separate? Can I break single elements into many parts and attach them to each other in a new alignment?

For example, a company that forges hot metal reversed two steps in its galvanizing process. The company not only solved a problem in quality control, it actually cut costs by about $1,500 a year. The production manager had simply changed the order of two production steps.

5. FIND THE ANALOGY

Try to look at old problems as if they were related to something with which you are more familiar. Dr. William Harvey, for example, became famous in medical history because he was the first man to explain how the circulatory system works. His discovery was based on a simple analogy. He thought of the heart as if it were a pump.

"Boss" Kettering, the prolific automotive inventor and engineer, once observed that in his field, creativity was dependent on the ability to "think the way the machine thinks."

These questions will help free your imagination to find an analogy:

What does this remind me of? What other things are like the elements of my problem? What is like this, only cheaper, quicker, easier? What can I borrow from another situation that I could apply to this one? In relation to this problem, can I treat it as if it were someone else's problem?

Consider how man solved the problem of flight. His first inspiration came from the flight of birds. That was his frame of reference. Only when scientists began to think of air as if it were water, did man break the frame of reference and actually fly. As you may know, modern aerodynamics is patterned after fluid dynamics.

6. CORRAL YOUR STRAY THOUGHTS

Ten thousand thoughts a day are yours without even asking. They just naturally occur to you. Unfortunately, most slip away before you ever have a chance to use them.

Only a few of these thoughts may ever help you solve a problem, but if you make a systematic attempt to retain all those which you *think* may help you solve a problem, you increase the chances of finding good ones you can use.

Corral stray thoughts by carrying a memo pad or notebook on your person. Keep a pad by your bed or dressing table at night. When thoughts occur, write them down.

Keep these tips in mind as you record your ideas and thoughts:

Get them down quickly, in the rough. Don't worry about details; you can fill them in later.

Review your recorded thoughts periodically, say, once a week. Separate the wheat from the chaff; discard those that don't look nearly as good on review as they did when you first put them down. Those that look good, try out on colleagues. Mark them for future consideration.

Finally, pay special attention to those ideas that recur. Perhaps you discarded a thought originally, but if it continues to pop up, there may be merit in it after all. Give it more serious consideration the second or third time around. The persistent thought is particularly valuable because it identifies your most perplexing problem.

7. PLAY IT CRAZY

Most people are afraid to do crazy things, to suggest crazy ideas. "People don't look often enough for the weird solution."

So says John Arnold, professor of creative engineering at M.I.T. Arnold plays it crazy in his classes. His students have to assume that they live on a planet where no normal frame of reference is permitted. Gravity is 11 times the strength of gravity on Earth; the atmosphere consists entirely of marsh gas; temperatures range from 122°F to 230°F; etc. Under such conditions, the students are forced to solve various engineering problems.

Arnold's students naturally produce some weird ideas, but having shed their conventional frames of reference and substituted new ones, they quickly acquire the habit of producing ideas that are practical for use right here on Earth.

Try out these questions to help you play it crazy:

If I could forget all the specifications, how else could the basic function be performed? Does it have to have a conventional conclusion? Conventional procedure? How much of what I am presently doing is the result of custom, tradition, opinion? What if I carry this to extremes? Will exaggeration help?

In the case of the M.I.T. students working to create solutions to problems in a crazy environment, they have engineered tractors with two engines—one for each track; a typewriter that can manipulate 4,000 symbols; unusual surgical instruments and household appliances; and many other similar engineering designs.

Of all the reference-shattering techniques named here, one may be enough to help you find the answer to solving your own problems of creativity. Perhaps you'll want to try two or three. You'll probably find, as most creative managers have, that there is more than one way through the maze.

Your creative subordinates

There are basically three kinds of creative people:

1. Those who *manage* creativity. You have just learned that it takes a somewhat creative manager and leader to stimulate creativity among the rank and file.

2. Those people who actually create new ideas and new things.

3. Those who re-arrange older ideas or older things, putting them in a new order or in a new perspective.

In a typical corporation, though there will be many people who are somewhat creative, creativity is found most often among the speech-writers, the advertising and public relations men, the men in new product development and marketing, and, of course, in the research and development laboratories. Less often, you may find a very creative man on your sales force or in the executive suite.

Such creative employees (as well as those that *seem* creative) require special study. William B. Lewis, chairman of the board of Kenyon & Eckhardt, a New York advertising agency, once put it this way in a speech:

> In dealing with creative people, remember always that they are among the gayest and moodiest, the brightest and stubbornest, the openest and most suspicious, the quickest-witted and slowest-moving, the most delightful and most exasperating people in the whole world.
>
> The trick is to know when and how to approach them, and indeed even how you look at them. A casual glance of no significance whatever has been

known to throw a creative man into a blue funk for
24 hours.

But don't let them fool you, these creative people. As a rule,
they are surrounded by a mystique that has a tendency to wipe
out objectivity and cloud management perception.

The myths about creativity

If the truth were but known, you would find that creative
people are often ordinary people with some extraordinary gifts.
They are subject to the same rules of human behavior as the rest
of us. Whatever aura they carry about with them can be easily
dispelled by a few simple facts. In the cold light of objectivity,
then, let's explore the mystique—and explode it:

1. *Belief:* That creative people are very intelligent.

   Truth: This is not necessarily so. Creativity can be found
in individuals of average intellectual functioning. A man may be
a creative genius without being a genius.

2. *Belief:* That creative people are "born that way" (or are
"naturally creative").

   Truth: People can be trained to be creative. People *learn*
to be creative—they are not born with the creative instinct. A
1959 study at the University of Buffalo indicated that a course
in creative problem-solving produced a significant increment on
certain ability measures. The psychologist Irving M. Maltzman
has shown at U.C.L.A. that people can be taught in many ways
how to create new ideas and new solutions to old problems.

3. *Belief:* That all creative people are highbrow, cultured,
artists and musicians.

   Truth: Patently false. You'll find creative talent among
garden variety housewives. The typical mother, for example, who
finds new ways to organize her work, new ways to place her
living room furniture, new ways to vary a basic recipe, can be
considered creative. People can find new ways to be creative
in their work (although functioning in essentially non-creative
jobs) and in their personal lives.

The potential for creativity is in each of us. For example, an article in *Time* Magazine describes how an English housewife ("a short, roly poly fortyish divorcee") invented a typewriter that types music—something that composers and musicians have wanted, but couldn't develop, for centuries. The inventor, Lily Pavey, was a former circus clown. She hit on her bright idea one day while working as an invoice clerk, got the inspiration for a technical breakthrough while riding in a creaky elevator, then spent 14 years perfecting her invention. She had only a year and a half of formal schooling, and did all her experimenting in a cluttered flat in South London. The experiments were financed by winnings from soccer pools, donations from friends, and a small foundation grant.

I say again — the potential for creativity is in all of us.

4. *Belief:* That creative people are usually older, in full bloom of seniority.

Truth: There is much evidence to the contrary. Dr. Harvey C. Lehman, an Ohio State University professor, has identified outstanding leaders in chemistry, mathematics, philosophy, literature, art, education, and public life, all of whom reached a peak of creativity prior to the age of 45, and occasionally in their 30's. Lehman further concludes that the curve of creativity in the individual rises rapidly in early maturity, then declines slowly after attaining an early maximum. And Lehman's work was done before the Kennedy era, which emphasized creative talent in youth.

5. *Belief:* That creative people are undisciplined and disorderly.

Truth: The creative person is very disciplined and orderly. He may give an outward appearance of disorderliness, but in his own mind, he is usually very organized.

Most experts in creativity now agree with N.Y.U. Professor Morris Stein, a foremost authority in this field. Stein believes that the creative person must resolve himself to having the fruits of his creation meet basic public criteria and thus be acceptable, useful, and satisfying to others. In other words, creativity must eventually pass the test of public judgment, and creative people know this. Therefore, their creative productions are reasonably well-organized.

6. *Belief:* That creative people must be left alone to wait for inspiration.

Truth: False: Creative people, like others, need to be left alone at times. But creative people also need work disciplines. There are many famous artists and writers who admit, "If I had to wait until inspiration came, I'd never get my work done." The inspiration for creativity comes only rarely, and sometimes never. Most creative geniuses put themselves on work schedules— long, hard hours. They force themselves to create. James Gould Cozzens, a two-finger typist, worked from eight a.m. to noon for *eight years* to write, *"By Love Possessed."* "For every three pages I wrote," he says, "I threw away two. On a good day, I got two pages done."

Creativity almost never comes suddenly, like a bolt out of the blue. It is hard work. Many people are taught that Newton sat under an apple tree, an apple fell on his head, and Newton thus discovered the law of gravity; or that Archimedes jumped out of the bathtub and proclaimed, "Eureka, I now know that a body displaces its own weight in water;" that Watt looked at his grandma's tea kettle and said, "Hey, Grandma, I just discovered the steam engine."

All these beliefs are untrue. Nobody invented the steam engine by watching a tea kettle. These discoveries did not occur without tremendous preparation and mental discipline. The great discoverers and inventors of history were precise in their thinking and well-directed in their activity. The great artists of history did not produce their best work while secluded in a dingy apartment, coughing up the blood of tuberculosis, dying in the arms of a mink-clad banker's daughter. The great artists of history, some of whom were not particularly inspired, trained themselves to create and worked at it constantly.

Another point on the mystique of creativity. If you are one of those who believes that a person is creative because he studied in Paris for a year, or because he lives in a garret in Greenwich Village, you're wrong. He may have the *trappings* of creativity, but he's not creative until he meets the public's standards. As Peter Drucker has pointed out on numerous occasions, you don't need the torn clothing, scraggly beard and the often neurotic manifestations of creativity in order to create. You can be just as creative in a grey flannel suit.

Naturally, in some respects creative people *are* different. Without dwelling at length on why creative people merit special treatment by management, I'll just name a few of the reasons:

1. Creative people, primarily because of their talent, are highly desirable in any company, thus frequently the hardest to recruit and hold.

2. Creative people are often at their best when they break the rules—extending or neglecting policy, misinterpreting or neglecting instructions.

3. Creative people may chafe at working with others, especially with others who aren't creative.

4. Creative people may respond differently to your criticism, praise, motivation, leadership and other approaches that less creative employees generally accept.

5. Creative people sometimes have gaps in their knowledge, or possess personal idiosyncracies, that others find hard to understand. Thus, in some circumstances, creative people may become a focus of conflict among your workers.

How to stimulate creativity

Now, what can a manager do to stimulate creativity? How much pressure should management exert?

Dr. Jules D. Porsche, a research manager with Armour & Co. of Chicago, has an answer. He points out that you have to exert *some* pressure on creative people to discipline them; how *much* pressure, depends.

If you are working toward a short-term goal with your creative subordinates, and want to inspire them just for the moment, then you should create a moderate amount of tension and pressure. However, for truly creative long-term productivity, an increase in tension and pressure will only frustrate your subordinates and you had best back off—use pressure with caution. Of course, points out Porsche, you have to be able to afford the patience required to wait for unpressured, long-range creativity.

To stimulate creativity in others, whether they be presently creative or merely aspiring to be creative, you have to provide a creative climate, one that is receptive and conducive to new ideas. Moreover, assuming that the creative worker has an adequate background of factual knowledge in his field of work, he must still be thoroughly familiar with the policy framework in which he must operate.

The creative person must also be motivated. He must be restless. You rarely see an idea man who is complacent, self-satisfied, happy with his current situation. He needs ants in his pants, a thorn in his flesh. However, research has shown that this compelling force must not be intermixed with frustration, anxiety, or fear. The compelling force in the creative person must be a positive attitude, in contrast with the defensive attitude found in the fearful or frustrated person. The man with fearful motivations is more likely to "play it safe" than to look for creative plays. Therefore, if you are trying to make your subordinates more creative, don't threaten them. You will get resistance, not results.

In addition, the creative person must see a clearly recognized need for the product of his creativity· He must believe that you need what he can produce. A research scientist will produce a new product for market only if he recognizes the public's need (or perhaps the need of the company to find a way to beat its competitor).

Finally, make sure that your creative subordinates understand the exact nature of the problem they are trying to solve, whether it be in research, sales, production, or anything else. Be as precise as possible in defining the problem; otherwise, solutions may be off-target. Will Rogers once said that he and Bernard Baruch both knew that the world was all wrong, but neither of them knew what to do about it. He meant that in jest, but the truth is, neither Rogers nor Baruch knew *exactly* what was wrong with the world. If they did, perhaps they could have suggested something helpful.

Most authorities agree on one general point: In managing creativity, good supervision is the critical factor. The creative man's relationship with his immediate superior overshadows every other influence.

Successful supervisors of creative activity suggest these rules as the most important ones in managing creative people:

1. GEAR THE PRESSURE TO GOALS

Many creative people, as Porsche puts it, "need the reassurance of gentle pressure on the reins." You have to maintain just enough pressure to keep the subordinate constantly aware of his objective.

This is different from the kind of pressure that forces haste or constant concentration. The creative man often works best in fits and starts. Even when this is not so, there must always be a certain amount of latitude for him to work at his own pace. Fixing some definite goals and an approximate time limit will help to provide the needed sense of urgency.

2. MAINTAIN CONTACT

"Warm, encouraging acceptance on the part of the supervisor always stimulates creative output," says Porsche. Or, as Dr. Donald Pelz of the University of Michigan puts it, "Creative performance is highest when supervision provides an intermediate degree of independence." That is, contact must never be lost between the individual and his superior.

Frequent communication, coupled with freedom to make certain decisions alone, appears to be the ideal compromise. It should be readily apparent to any good supervisor or executive that creative people need a sympathetic ear, someone who listens and comments enough to help them nail down their conclusions.

3. LET HIM KNOW WHERE HE STANDS

Guidance must be supplied: constructive criticism, for example, or praise for good work. The creative man hungers for evaluation of his efforts. The problem is, appraisal of creative efforts is often difficult because results may be indefinite or long-postponed. Special care should be taken, therefore, to:

● Watch for signs of brooding resentment, even more than for outright complaints.

● Talk informally with each creative person from time to time, demonstrating your interest in his problems.

● Define over-all objectives and indicate that you know what he is seeking.

● Let him know the importance of his results when they finally do come in.

● Convey the reactions of customers and others whenever such information becomes available.

4. DEFEND HIM AGAINST THE ATTACKS OF OTHERS

There is a limit to how much of a guardian angel a creative man deserves. But the nature of his job may make it wise to tolerate some of his shortcomings: lateness, absenteeism, or his impatience with other people, for example.

In your defense of him, make the most of his accomplishments, especially if he has already contributed to the welfare of others. Make these two points: First, the inconsistency of his habits is necessary to his achievement of valuable ideas. Second, his impatience with others comes from deep absorption in a task, not from personal animosity. In some cases, of course, you may not be able to explain away his peculiarities or tardiness. Your only consolation is that creative people are sometimes misunderstood.

Under no circumstances should you fabricate excuses for your creative personnel. Nor should you tolerate an excessive amount of tardiness and other minor faults. Don't let the mystique of creativity cloud your vision. Remember, creative people are ordinary people. They need disciplines, too.

5. GIVE THE CREATIVE PERSON SOME TIME ALONE

Many of a creative man's best ideas occur to him during an idle period immediately following periods of intense concentration. That's when his unconscious mind presents his conscious mind with insight and illumination.

Supreme Court Justice William O. Douglas realizes the value in this. "When writing a book or a lecture," he once wrote about himself in *The New York Times*, "I have often come to a cul-de-sac, the next terminal being hidden from view. Or an argued case has projected difficult questions that loom so large that no opinion can be written until they are resolved. While my conscious processes are engaged [in hiking, searching out trees and birds], the subconscious is solving my professional or personal problems. It is seldom that all perplexities are not clarified by the end of 20 miles. Answers and solutions, previously bothersome, become clear as day."

Moreover, while it is true that the individual whose creative effort is part of a group project develops ideas later, when he is alone and experimenting, the reverse is also true. Several creative people coming together *after* individual study stimulate each other's thinking and accomplish more than they could individually. In either event, the point is made that 100 per cent group creativity projects don't work except in the case of brainstorming, which is a one-shot, short-term event.

6. MAKE HIM SECURE

Any person whose contribution is principally in the realm of ideas rather than action, is normally at his best when only his mind, not his security or self, is challenged. You must encourage him to build his self-confidence to the maximum.

"No creative individual," says Dr. Edwin Tolman, "can function well when he is too frightened, too insecure, too emotional or too anything else." The problem to be solved creates sufficient tension. So, pay your creative personnel well, give them security and satisfaction in their jobs, grant any reasonable requests that they make.

7. SHOW TOLERANCE FOR FAILURE

A creative atmosphere requires that a man be able to present radical, even unworkable, ideas without being harshly judged. The best new product your company ever produced might have sounded like a ridiculous joke when it was first proposed.

Remember, all ideas aren't good ideas. When you ask a man to experiment with ideas and innovate and create, you must give him an even greater margin for error than you give others. If you don't, his fear of failure will prevent true initiative. Remember that, for the truly creative man, many apparent failures are merely steps to the eventual success.

8. RESPECT HIS OUTSIDE ACTIVITIES AND SOURCES OF STIMULATION

The creative thinker must be free to communicate with peers having useful knowledge, points of view, and ideas of their own, in order that he may refresh himself. In addition, he may need professional status by identifying with an elite that transcends business and industry.

Thus, the creative person often seeks involvement in non-company activities with non-company people: professional societies, community affairs, attendance at conventions, lecturing or writing for specialized audiences. Many firms are inclined to discourage such associations on the basis that they sap some of the individual's energies. This is the wrong approach.

You must recognize that a man's creative needs may not be wholly satisfied within the company. When it becomes apparent, however, that outside activities are interfering with completion of work tasks and responsibilities to the firm, of course they should be curbed.

9. PROVIDE SPECIAL DIRECTION

The creative person needs "propositional" leadership—that is, the middle road between firmness and permissiveness. Peter Drucker cites the example of opera managers whose ability to handle gifted vocal artists in as essential to success as is the talent of the singers. "A successful opera manager," he says, "is one who thinks of prima donnas not as a nuisance, but as an asset that he is paid to govern well."

On the other hand, you cannot pamper the creative person; he would become the spoiled brat of the company. As the administrator of a top research team once told me, "I have to distinguish between the inventive man's impatience with unrealized possibilities, and mere petulance over failure."

10. PROVIDE A CREATIVE ATMOSPHERE

No man can produce new ideas and creative solutions to problems when he is working in an uncomfortable environment. Management should, therefore, try to make its creative personnel feel at home by placing them in an environment conducive to creative thought.

For instance, you might relieve creative people of performing routine chores that they claim are "beneath" them—and which could be performed less expensively and just as well by non-creative personnel. Filling out reports is one example. Also, it is a good idea to provide creative personnel with conveniences that make their jobs easier, thus freeing their minds for free flight and imaginative thought. Finally, consider the physical environment—the visual and acoustical factors, the physical comforts.

11. RECOGNIZE CREATIVITY

Creative people like to feel that they are "something special," worthy of extra consideration. To the extent that management's consideration, acknowledgement, and recognition of creativity brings results, this is highly desirable.

In an engineering department of the Eastman Kodak Co., for example, management takes several steps to recognize the special status of the creative engineers:

● The salary structure recognizes different levels of creative performance.

● Individuals are given the opportunity to talk about current achievements to their peers, both at Kodak and at professional or technical societies.

● Unusual accomplishments are publicized in the organization's newsletters.

● Engineers are encouraged to obtain professional licenses, and are provided the means to prominently display them at their work stations.

12. DON'T DEMAND TOTAL CREATIVITY, EITHER OF YOURSELF OR OF ANYONE ELSE

This is particularly critical when *hiring* creative people. Don't seek people who are wholly creative. A man who has talents in addition to creativity is to be preferred, even if his creative talent is slightly lessened.

David Ogilvy touched on this point in his book, *Confessions of an Advertising Man.* Ogilivy, a creative genius who founded and now heads one of the most respected agencies in advertising, says, "It is usually useless to be wholly creative. In addition to being an original thinker, you must be able to sell what you create. Management cannot be expected to recognize a good idea unless it is presented by a good salesman."

13. WHEN SOLICITING CREATIVE IDEAS AND SUGGESTIONS, EVALUATE THEM QUICKLY

Creative people are even more impatient than executives. They like to have their ideas and creative work evaluated quickly. That makes sense from a creative productivity point of view, too. One reason why the military establishment is so lacking in imagination is because ideas and suggestions take too long to reach the stage of judgment.

"The loneliest man in the military is the man with new ideas," says Col. Charles F. Austin, who has a Ph.D. from Harvard and teaches at the U. S. Army Management School. "The chain of command stifles creative thought by taking too long to act on suggestions. Nothing will discourage an enthusiastic suggestor sooner than to have to wait months to get results. I know of a post where the suggestion has been sarcastically made that an effort be made to process suggestions sometime during the present tour of military personnel submitting them."

14. DON'T DENY CREATIVE PEOPLE THEIR INNOCENT AND HARMLESS FOIBLES

Such things are likely to cost management little or nothing, and yet they may be critical to creative functioning. I know a speechwriter for a major public figure who cannot write a word unless he puts a full pitcher of ice water next to his typewriter—no glass, just a pitcher!

Such harmless quirks are known to psychologists as sensory cues; they cue the creative man's senses and act as stimulants. The smell of rotten apples in his desk stimulated Schiller, the German poet and playwright; when concentrating on metaphysical problems, Kant focused on a tower seen through his window; Freud used cheroots as a stimulant.

David Ogilvy once said:

Many people, and I think I'm one of them, are more productive and more fertile when they've had a little to drink. I find that if I drink two or three brandies, or a good bottle of claret, I'm far better able to write. I also find that if I listen to music, this loosens me up.

A *victim of conflict*

I would not be surprised if, despite all this discussion, the actual management of creativity still seems difficult. Don't be disheartened.

The fact is, the creative man is a victim of sharp conflict in society's values.

First, there is emphasis on the integration of the individual into the group and its activities; then, there is a nurturing of the individual's creative talent. All evidence points to the fundamental incompatibility of these opposed values and goals.

As the Carnegie Corporation of New York pointed out in a research report on creativity:

> Creative talent has always existed and managed to flower. It will continue to do so. But if we want positively to encourage it, actively to nurture it, the conflict must be settled in favor of the individual. Such a settlement will come only when, as a society, we come more generally to understand that, if a man seems out of step with his fellows, it may be because, as Thoreau said, "He hears a different drummer. Let him step to the music which he hears, however measured or far away."

12.

How to Use
Competition to Get
Better Results

The competitive spirit in man has always been of vital interest to serious students of human behavior. Not only psychologists, but also psychiatrists—indeed, all social scientists—have studied competition for generations.

Over the years, two schools of thought have developed. One believes that competition is inherently destructive, and the other believes that competition is the stimulant of life.

Why you shouldn't use competition

This essentially negative consideration of competition is generally shared by theoreticians, scholars, and philosophers. And, historically, it has been the dominant school of thought.

For example, here's what the Spanish philosopher Gracian has to say about competition:

> Never compete. Every rivalry damages a competitor's credit. Competitors take every opportunity to belittle their adversaries in order to show them in a poor light. There are few who fight fairly; rivals discover faults that courtesy would forget. *The best of competition begets or revives dormant infamies and uncovers passed and forgotten scandals.*

Any executive who has ever competed for higher office, or any man who has ever fought in a political campaign, knows the truth in this. Some opponents will drag *everything* into a fray in order to win the contest. So that's Exhibit A against competition.

Exhibit B is a list of five highly critical, negative aspects of competition on which many psychologists agree. Psychologists say that competition often:

1. Creates much jealousy and animosity among employees.

2. Results in sharp criticism of fellow employees (leading to further animosity).

3. Starts false propaganda and rumor, including gossip.

4. Causes old employees to greet new workers coolly, meaning that new employees rarely get into the swing of things very quickly.

5. Causes employees to hoard their information, to withhold ideas for themselves, to be greedy about giving credit.

Some psychologists, in fact, don't stop their challenge with these five points. Dr. Gardner Murphy, director of research at the famed Menninger Clinic, once pointed out in a speech that extreme competition can be terribly destructive. "Over-competitiveness," he said, "manifests itself in the increased strain . . . in the perpetual effort to justify one's self, to be right, to win a victory where we all can't come out ahead."

I also want to point out here still another negative consideration. Often, you may not be able to get people to engage in a competitive contest. For some, a competitive contest is a demotivator. Unless people know they have at least a 50-50 chance of winning, they won't even bother to play the game. Withdrawal at least protects them from the risk of failure.

As I noted in a report I helped to prepare for the Research Institute of America:

> People who don't see much chance of success cannot be inveigled into making an effort. Any teacher knows that children who work for scholastic honors are only the few who feel a possibility of winning. The rest of the children sit back and let the competi-

tors work—while the non-competitors go about business of their own choosing. This may be very
frustrating in children but adults behave in the same
way. Competition in your company may fail to motivate your people for the same reason.

A president of a public utility recently told me, after distribu-
ting almost a half-million dollars in across-the-board salary increases: "You know, I doubt if we will obtain any benefit from the
increases except to keep us up with other companies. Our weakest
people feel it's coming to them, our strongest individuals work
hard anyway for their own personal fullfillment. Most important,
the broad middle group that could be stimulated by a merit increase feels somewhat let down. But if I were to put all my eggs
in merit raises and make everyone compete, a handful of people
may take the whole pot of gold. Maybe," he said as he scratched
his head, "competition causes more problems than it solves."

Why you should use competition

But competition is not all bad. It cannot be dispensed with
so easily.

For, despite all that the theoreticians tell us, the men of action
know differently. The younger school of thought, the movers of
society, the executives and managers of corporate business, believe
strongly in the power of competition. Men are selected for jobs on
the basis of competitive tests; men are paid for competing against
each other or against quotas or goals; many a success has been
attributed to the hot breath of the competition close behind.
Indeed, our nation's enterprise and economy is built on competition.

Clarence Randall, former head of Inland Steel, put it succinctly
when he said: "In the management of a business the sharp bite
of honest aggressive competition is the automatic corrective measure to safeguard the public from extortion. A man cannot be making too much profit if others are trying to beat him at his own
game."

So competition, in Randall's view a system of checks and bal-
ances, really has much in favor as well as much in opposition.
Where is the resolution of this conflict? Is competition a boon or
a detriment to our business society? Is it a deadly sin or a virtue?

Sociologist Margaret Mead once said that most Americans are "conflicted about competition." They believe, she said, that competition is generally good, but that it is not good for *you*. To illustrate her point, she explained how most mothers like to feel that their children will stand up for themselves; yet, they don't want their kids to hit other kids.

In business, my feeling is that it is possible for executives to use competition, and to do so effectively, in a less destructive fashion than that gloomily preached by some men of "academia." I believe it is possible *to cooperate with others in a competitive manner*.

There is, in my opinion, no sharp line of differentiation between cooperation and competition. These two concepts overlap considerably. It is possible, therefore, to become cooperative within a framework of competition—to use competition constructively, as managers and as individuals.

Achieving competition without hostility

A very real danger, one that you should recognize, is that the average businessman may inadvertently confuse cooperation and competition, especially when he is under pressure to "get the job done." There is much about competition and cooperation that is disarmingly similar, and confusing. Goal-setting is an example.

But it is possible to stimulate yourself and others to play the game of competition in a friendly manner; to compete with strength and vigor, but in a sportsmanlike fashion; to play rough and tough, but fairly and according to the rules of the game. By so doing, you can avoid most of the consequences that you have just been warned about.

In the following pages we will find out just how competition, as an aggressive component of personality, can be utilized more effectively. I shall point out the dangers of extreme individual competition, rules for playing the game, and, of course, some practical methods by which you can use this very important and effective tool.

The dangers of extreme individual competition

First, I want to clear the air by pointing out that there are three kinds of competition: individual pitted against individual, group against group, and the individual against himself. The first is the most troublesome; the other two present fewer difficulties and are therefore more likely to be productive.

I frequently tell this story to illustrate the troublesome nature of individual competition. One day I was playing golf with a top executive. Like most executives, he is extremely competitive and has intense desire for success. But on this occasion, because I am not a good golfer, he was coaching and counseling me on nearly every hole: which club to use, how to hold the club, and how to play the shot. Naturally, being the better golfer, he was beating me all the way.

On one short, par three hole I was lucky enough to get on the green with my tee shot. I was lined up for a birdie. My teacher, meanwhile, had driven his ball into the woods. He suddenly underwent a complete change in personality. No longer my teacher, he became my *competitor*. He became angry. In fact, he wanted to bet me that, even though he had botched his first shot, he would do as well as I on the hole. For the remainder of the round I didn't get so much as one more word of helpful advice. His whole role changed.

I wouldn't say that hostility grew up between us, but certainly for the last few holes our relationship was a troublesome one. That's what often happens when individuals compete against each other.

What happens when a manager intentionally stimulates competition among his subordinates? Some hostility is bound to be created. Moreover, when the manager intentionally pits one man against another ("Here, Sam. Look at Joe's work. Can you do better than this? There may be a bonus in it for you."), hostility can get completely out of hand.

I was once told by the vice-president of a large rubber company, "Yes, I believe in competition. It's good. But frankly, it is so full of dynamite that we are frightened to explore its maximum potential." Similarly, the director of employee communications for a petroleum corporation told me, "We strive to eliminate competition. It's like nuclear energy; it could blow the place apart and wreck everything. Since we're not sure we can control it, we are unwilling to play with it."

Psychologists and sociologists, working under the direction of Dr. Gordon Allport as a special subcommittee of the Social Science Research Council, have studied the mechanisms of competition. They point out that competition often whips up fear of one's own ability to cope with the presence of threat, and the fear then emerges in the form of hostility against others.

In that process, certain side-effects are produced:

1. *Jealousy.* Approbation, approval, rewards to others, are now interpreted as personal threats. There is no rejoicing in the ranks when someone is praised. Each subordinate is more likely to want to "get" the other, to keep him in his place, to prevent him from advancing.

2. *Distortion.* The hostility causes people to draw away from one another. Each individual becomes over-sensitive, distorts and misinterprets the behavior of his fellow employees.

3. *Sharp criticism.* There is very little praise and much critical evaluation among competing individuals. In a climate of extreme competition, any mild error is harshly called to the attention of others.

4. *Rumors.* Wild stories are taken at face value and the game of shop politics goes on to a greater extent in competitive groups.

5. *Coolness toward new employees.* Fear of the outsider is increased. The new recruit gets no help from the old-timers. Little attempt is made to integrate him into the work group.

6. *Holding back.* No one talks up a good idea; there is a withholding, for fear of losing credit. This also results in people running to the managers with half-baked ideas that would have benefited from a freer give-and-take in open discussion with some colleagues.

7. *Duplication.* Where competition exists on an individual basis, there is bound to be duplication of effort. Subordinates who feel competitive toward each other prefer to do a job from scratch, rather than use the work already done by the rival.

8. *Cracking under pressure.* Faced with the problem of achievement in limited time, subordinates in a competitive situation are less able to organize themselves to get the work done efficiently.

9. *Quantity.* Production is erratic, moving in extreme up-and-down swings. Output may go up when the pressure is on, but later a reaction sets in and the benefits are often washed away. The energy reserve of subordinates is drained by the tension of competition and little is left for the regular everyday work.

10. *Quality.* Even if quantity does go up, according to studies by Dr. John F. Dashiell, a heavy price is paid in loss of quality.

Ten rules for playing the game

But if, as I've said, competition is not all that bad, what can be done to make the most of its *positive* effects? How can you avoid the unpleasant consequences of competition? Try using competition according to these basic rules. In the past when I have recommended them, they have worked very effectively.

1. *Choose a "safe" battleground.* It is not safe to whip up individual competition unless the work situation is relatively normal. It's unwise to turn on the competitive heat in times of rapid personnel turnover, mass hiring or layoffs, salary adjustments, or changes in equipment requiring retraining, for example.

In times of extreme tension, people will respond negatively to any additional strain. A contest to beat out other employees may be just enough to destroy previously good human relations. You may require years to put the pieces together again. Don't risk it. Make sure a healthy state of morale exists at the time the competition begins.

2. *Choose an impersonal target.* Look over the negative reactions to competition I spoke of earlier. That's what you want to prevent. Most of them, as I pointed out, are the by-products of hostility; such hostility can develop in three different directions:

- Toward other individuals in the company.
- Toward people outside the company.
- Toward an inanimate or impersonal object.

Margaret Mead points out that effective competition is most difficult to achieve when the competitive object is close emotionally—that the best competition results when the opponent, adversary, or goal is an external object to which there is no emotional attachment.

The wise manager directs the hostility towards inanimate objects and away from people. The impersonal target provides a safe outlet for aggressions and arouses no feeling of personal guilt.

For example, it's perfectly safe to hate accidents or waste. The fellow who wins the award doesn't threaten anybody's personal self-esteem because the victor has merely beaten the common enemy. All of the other contestants can enjoy the triumph.

The foe can be a quota or record that you want to break, a standard you want to improve, a clock you want to beat—any target other than a human being. That accounts for the particular success of competition between departments. It works in such contests as safety, waste and scrap control, incentive wage systems, and quality control.

3. *Put a time limit on the competition.* A competitive atmosphere is most productive when it is limited to a specified period. A contest, a program providing for individual recognition, should end on a given date. The time limit should be announced and clearly recognized by all.

Don't let the immediate positive results tempt you into extending the date indefinitely once a limit has been announced. You are likely to run into the point of diminishing returns, and may kill off the constructive use of competition for the future.

4. *Keep tabs on what's happening.* Don't allow the competition to run wild. Even under the best of circumstances, even if you follow all the soundest principles, it may result in chaos unless you are constantly watching the reactions of your people. Vigilance is necessary to prevent a major explosion. The supervisor must keep an eye on every competitor to make certain that fair play is guaranteed at all times, undercutting is prevented, insults against other employees are discouraged, and rumors and petty politics do not get out of hand.

In the effort to win, people may be tempted to shove fellow-employees out of the way. Underhanded maneuvering and the seizing of opportunities to give someone else a verbal black eye may increase suddenly and at an alarming rate. This is one case where it's wise to watch the pot so that it doesn't bubble over.

5. *Remain above the battle.* Don't take sides. The competition must be free and open. You have to keep your own prejudices and preferences in check.

Avoid anything that might be interpreted as favoritism to any of the competitors. Make it clear that everyone starts out with a clean slate; no one has any advantage, and no one is carrying a handicap as a result of previous performance records.

6. *Communicate progress.* Whenever possible, report how things are going. Results should be publicly posted so that eve ry-one can see where he stands. Bulletin boards, house organs, or special memos may be used. Sometimes, charts, barometers, or horse racing symbols can be used tc give a light touch.

It is essential that progress charts be kept up to date. Waiting too long to post results often causes enthusiasm to wane.

One trucking firm, for example, ran a successful contest to reduce time lost on the road without increasing accidents. Attractive posters were made up for the various dispatchers' offices to keep interest high. Careful steps were taken to make sure that results were promptly communicated. In some cases, phone calls were made to diners where the truck drivers were known to stop so that they could get the latest standings immediately.

7. *Set goals with built-in yardsticks.* "Individual competition," a supervisor in a glass fibre company remarked, "can be a real boon to production. But don't fool yourself into believing you can excite people into competition without specific goals and standards."

The competitors have to know exactly where they are going and they must know and understand exactly how their progress will be measured. Without specific goals, there can be no motivation. And without yardsticks to measure achievement, morale will suffer.

This holds true not only in contests but in every kind of situation where people feel they are competing with each other. Even if the only objective of the competitors is to rate higher in your esteem, you owe it to them to specify your standards.

8. *Provide face-saving devices.* Even with the best rules and the most skillful application, some sensitive subordinates are likely to come out with bruised feelings. You have to set up an emotional first aid station.

Make it your business, in every competitive situation, to reassure the loser that he is still an important and essential part of your work team. No one can win all the time, and the employee's value to you is not diminished by the fact that someone else has come in first.

Whatever the employees may be competing for—first prize in a contest, a promotion, a better assignment, more pay under an incentive plan—remember that people want a later chance to make a fresh start. Give the winner his reward or his recognition, but don't play up the hero too long. That's the surest way to make him disliked and end his usefulness.

9. *Be humane, humble, and grateful.* Similarly, if you yourself are involved in a competitive situation and emerge as the winner, adopt an attitude which the loser can regard with respect. Don't say, "My success is your failure." If you do, surely you will lose whatever support he can give you.

On the other hand, if you share your prestige and your winnings, you may enlist his support to help you continue to win and stay on top. This is one reason why the Kennedy family, a highly competitive clan, is so much loved despite the fact that its members win in nearly every competition they enter. The Kennedys operate under the concept, "We will share with you the result of our common effort, even though I won, even though I am the leader."

(If you have on your staff persons who are consistent winners in competitive situations, be sure to counsel them on this point, as well as on the one that follows.)

10. *Never demean the loser.* The loser has lost. He feels his loss keenly. Don't demean him and irritate him by gloating over your victory. If you do, you will merely increase the chances of stirring up his hostility. Don't even gloat in a light or humorous vein; don't mock. It may come out sounding like sarcasm.

I have a hunch that one of the reasons why some psychiatrists and psychologists have such negative attitudes toward competition is because they are more likely to see the losers who have been demeaned. They rarely see the winners, and they rarely see the losers who have been helped by victorious but understanding opponents.

When you irritate and demean a person by calling attention to his failure, the world may become so threatening to him that he may never enter competition again. His ego can be destroyed. His effectiveness is lessened.

I remember when I was a young biology student, our class conducted laboratory experiments with the hydra, a jelly-like organism that puts out tentacles. If we pricked the hydra with a pin, providing stimulation, it would put out a tentacle in the direction of the prick. But if we pricked it too often or caused too much damage to the hydra, it would send out nothing. In fact, it would coagulate into a hard core.

I draw this analogy to illustrate a point. When it comes to competition, *stimulate but don't irritate.* If the competition is stimulating, your subordinates act. If it is irritating, they do nothing. No organism wants to expose itself to possible failure and continued irritation.

Practical advice on using competition in groups

Competition between groups, as compared to competition between individuals, is not only a lot easier to manage, it carries considerably less danger of hostility. Moreover, it offers you an opportunity to observe the leaders of the groups in a competitive situation, without exposing them to many of the dangers of an individual competition.

The armed services recognize this. Military officers deliberately try to create in each unit the feeling that "we're the best damn outfit in the best damn army." A traditional rivalry between different branches of the military, kept alive by separate uniforms and insignia, has proved to be a powerful motivating force.

In business, similar rivalries between departments can be constructive. However, though less dangerous than individual competition, group competition still requires proper policing.

Competition between two departments may be undesirable when the departments are dependent for their success on a high degree of cooperation. In such cases, it may be best to avoid competition and the possibility of friction.

For example, a race between the day shift and the night shift may seem a natural. Better check first. Is there any danger that one shift will be tempted to leave equipment in poor condition and thus reduce the productivity of the others? If you do have competition, you must take special pains to guard against this danger.

As a general rule, you will find that group competition works best in three basic situations:

1. *With relatively independent units.* Of course, every group in the same company is linked to every other in some way. But the interdependence is a matter of degree.

In most cases where the purpose of competition is to raise *output*, departments that function without too much cooperation from each other can be involved. For example, tool room vs. shipping, or maintenance vs. shipping.

The subject matter of the competition may also determine which are the most suitable departments. If you are launching a contest on attendance, fund-raising, or housekeeping, the interdependence of the departments will not ordinarily matter.

2. *Where a common enemy exists.* It's usually safe to pit group against group when both realize that they are fighting a common enemy. Teams can be set in competition with each other for the stated purpose of outmaneuvering the company's principal competitor. This can be done, for instance, with campaigns to work up ideas for improving customer service, or perhaps to cut costs and thus make possible a price reduction.

Sometimes the common enemy may be an aspect of the job that the employees dislike. You might want to invite competition on how to eliminate certain boring jobs or how to reduce unscheduled overtime work.

Your objective should be to make the triumph only incidentally a victory of one group over the other. The real victory should be *the conquest of the problem* so that everybody still benefits, regardless of which team comes up with the answer.

3. *Where creative thinking is needed.* Sometimes it's desirable

to put two teams to work in competition with each other and to cut off all contact between them. This is likely to be the case if you need original thinking and experimentation.

Military research makes frequent use of this type of competition. The United States Navy obtained good results when it commissioned General Electric and Westinghouse to work separately on the atomic-powered submarine. Communication between the two firms was actively discouraged. Admiral Hyman Rickover, director of the project, didn't care about duplication or repetition of error. He wanted diverse thinking and, if possible, different solutions.

Westinghouse came up with the first answer in the Nautilus, but a great deal was learned from GE's atomic sub, the Sea Wolf.

This kind of competition is much easier where two independent companies are pitted against each other. But when the two teams are in the same firm, wholesome results can still be obtained by observing a few simple precautions:

Keep reminding each of the groups for which you are responsible that it is part of the whole company. Stress the fact that no matter which team wins, everybody—the company and its people —will benefit.

As in the case of individual competition, you must also bear in mind the importance of policing the rivalry to insure fairness, reporting progress regularly and frequently, and providing face-saving devices for the runner-up.

A case in point

I want to conclude this chapter with a short illustration of how the president of a large service company in New York is presently using competition effectively among individuals.

Late in 1964, the executive vice-president of this firm died. He knew he had cancer and was very concerned about who was going to succeed him when he bowed out. About a month before he retired, therefore, he wrote a letter to the president and made a suggestion.

"Here's how to fill my shoes," he wrote. "Don't immediately promote a man to this job. Instead, set up a competition. There are two bright and capable young men in this company who might qualify. Each man is now a supervisor. Make both of them vice-presidents, one in charge of production and the other in charge of sales.

"These men are good friends with each other. They will compete with each other for the next job up, the one I presently hold, the job we really want to fill. They will compete with all their strength, but they will not destroy the company; they will help the company because they will use their competition to pace each other.

"After a few years, see which man is doing the better job. Make him executive vice-president, for he will have proven himself worthy of the responsibility."

It was excellent advice.

As Amos Alonzo Stagg always believed, the purpose of competition is not to beat someone down, but to bring out the best in every player.

Index